Naoya Hatakeyama

NAOYA HATAKEYAMA

Edited by / Herausgegeben von Stephan Berg
Texts by / Texte von Stephan Berg, Charlotte Cotton, Naoya Hatakeyama

Hatje Cantz

Contents / Inhalt

7 Foreword
9 Vorwort
Stephan Berg, Ellen Seifermann, Els Barents

11 Down to the Waterline
17 Down to the Waterline
Stephan Berg

Illustrations / Abbildungen
23 Lime Works (Factory Series)
35 Lime Hills (Quarry Series)
49 Blast
59 River Series
71 Underground / River (Tunnel Series)
79 Underground / Water
89 Untitled
101 Untitled / Osaka
105 Still Life
117 Slow Glass

125 Away from Home
127 Fern von Zuhause
Charlotte Cotton

Appendix
131 Biography
131 Solo Exhibitions
132 Group Exhibitions
133 Public Collections
133 Selected Bibliography

Foreword

Naoya Hatakeyama is regarded in Japan as one of the leading photo artists of his generation. Since the mid-eighties, the photographer, who lives in Tokyo, has created an oeuvre focused in large measure on the dialectical relationship between nature and civilization. In his broad series of primarily of small-format photographs, *Lime Works (Factory Series)* from 1991 to 1994 and *Lime Hills (Quarry Series)* from 1986 to 1991—a study of the landscapes and architectures of limestone quarries—and *Blast*, in progress since 1995—featuring photos of detonations in quarries that evoke explosive, sculptural effects—nature appears as a raw material immersed in a magical light, a material that achieves its true purpose only through industrial transformation. From limestone, as an important ingredient in cement, Hatakeyama proceeds to an intensive investigation of urban architecture. Using Tokyo as his example, he creates equally complex and suggestive images of a principle of urbanism which, though a product of the human mind, eliminates people entirely from its visual worlds. Working with the bird's-eye perspective, from which the city assumes the appearance of a vast, horizonless totality beyond the grasp of our vision (*Untitled*, 1989–97), his camera works its way through the vertical canyons of the metropolis (*River Series*, 1993–94) until it reaches the ordinarily unseen depths of the city sewer system (*Underground*, 1999).

The constellations the camera reveals have a certain surreal, archaic quality: stockpiles of limestone have the look of stone-age landscapes or views of the moon. The gorges between the skyscrapers resemble canyons cast in concrete and the sewer system, with its stage-like lighting, calls to mind enchantingly illuminated caves, while suggesting at the same time a view into the depths of the camera lens, as a striking reminder that Hatakeyama's elaborate staged scenes are always reflections on a specific visual principle of photography.

This vertical, seemingly almost archaeological approach with which the artist explores the urban organism from the air down to the noxiously shimmering surfaces of the sewers is coupled with a horizontal principle that is expressed above all in the serial concept underlying these works. Here, time appears as the second important element in Hatakeyama's art. Hatakeyama's layer-by-layer penetration into the body of the city is revealed as the other side of a horizontal exploration of a suspended time in which images merge to form a total view that fundamentally denies the progress of time, insisting solely on the permanence of the momentary, on the simultaneity of moment and eternity.

We are very pleased to present this oeuvre, still relatively unknown in Europe, in a broad survey which also encompasses more recent works completed in 2001, in Germany and the Netherlands for the first time. Our thanks are due above all to Naoya Hatakeyama for his dedicated and painstaking work on behalf of these exhibition projects. We also wish to thank the state of Lower Saxony and the Niedersächsische Lottostiftung for their generous funding support. We are very grateful to the L.A. Galerie in Frankfurt on Main, and especially to Lothar Albrecht, for their extensive organizational support, and to Hatje Cantz Publishers, who have assisted us in editing and producing the comprehensive catalogue of works. Our thanks go as well to the many lenders who enriched the exhibition through loans of important works.

Stephan Berg, Kunstverein Hannover
Ellen Seifermann, Kunsthalle Nürnberg
Els Barents, Huis Marseille, Foundation for Photography, Amsterdam

Vorwort

Naoya Hatakeyama gehört in Japan zu den wichtigsten Fotokünstlern seiner Generation. Seit Mitte der achtziger Jahre hat der in Tokio lebende Fotograf ein Werk entwickelt, in dessen Zentrum der dialektische Zusammenhang zwischen Natur und Zivilisation steht. In den breit angelegten, vorwiegend kleinformatigen Serien der *Lime Works (Factory Series)* von 1991 bis 1994 und *Lime Hills (Quarry Series)* von 1986 bis 1991 – eine Auseinandersetzung mit den Architekturen und Landschaften von Kalksteinwerken – sowie den *Blast* seit 1995 – gleichermaßen plastisch und explosiv wirkende Aufnahmen von Sprengungen in Steinbrüchen – erscheint Natur als ein in magisches Licht getauchter Rohstoff, der seine wahre Bestimmung erst im industriellen Umwandlungsprozess erfährt. Vom Kalkstein als wichtigem Bestandteil von Zement führt der Weg in der Folgezeit zu einer intensiven Beschäftigung mit städtischer Architektur. Am Beispiel Tokios entstehen ebenso komplexe wie suggestive Bilder eines urbanistischen Prinzips, das, wiewohl vom Menschen hergestellt, diesen völlig aus seinen Bildwelten ausspart. Ausgehend von der Vogelperspektive, aus der sich die Stadt als eine unüberschaubare, horizontlose Totalität zeigt (*Untitled*, 1989–1997), arbeitet sich die Kamera durch die vertikalen Schluchten der Metropole (*River Series*, 1993/94) bis in die Tiefen der normalerweise unsichtbar bleibenden Ebene der Kanalisation (*Underground*, 1999).

Die Konstellationen, die die Kamera dabei entdeckt, tragen in sich sowohl etwas Surreales wie Archaisches: Kalksteinhalden wirken wie Steinzeitlandschaften oder Ansichten vom Mond. Die Hochhausschluchten erinnern an betonierte Canyons, und die bühnenhaft ausgeleuchtete Kanalisation erscheint als magisch erhellte Höhle, bisweilen aber auch wie der Blick in die Tiefe eines Kameraobjektivs, der beispielhaft verdeutlicht, wie sehr Hatakeyamas elaborierte Inszenierungen immer auch Reflexionen eines spezifisch fotografischen Bildprinzips sind.

Dem vertikalen, nahezu archäologisch anmutenden Vorgehen, das den städtischen Organismus vom Luftraum bis hin zu den giftig schimmernden Abwasseroberflächen der Kloaken erforscht, steht ein horizontales Prinzip zur Seite, das sich vor allem in der seriellen Anlage der Arbeiten ausdrückt. In ihm verwirklicht sich der Zeitaspekt als zweites wichtiges Element in der Arbeit Hatakeyamas. Das schichtweise Eindringen in den Stadtkörper erweist sich als Kehrseite der horizontalen Auslotung einer zum Stillstand gekommenen Zeit, in der sich die Bilder zu einem Überblick formieren, der im Grunde keine zeitliche Sukzession mehr kennt, sondern allein auf einer Permanenz des Augen-Blicklichen insistiert, auf einem Zugleich von Moment und Ewigkeit.

Wir freuen uns, dieses in Europa noch wenig bekannte Werk erstmals in einem breiten Überblick, der auch ganz aktuelle Arbeiten aus dem Jahr 2001 einschließt, in Deutschland und Holland vorstellen zu können. Unser Dank gilt zunächst Naoya Hatakeyama für seine engagierte und präzise Arbeit an den Ausstellungsprojekten. Darüber hinaus bedanken wir uns für großzügige finanzielle Unterstützung bei dem Land Niedersachsen und der Niedersächsischen Lottostiftung. Der L.A. Galerie in Frankfurt am Main, namentlich Lothar Albrecht, sind wir für vielfältige organisatorische Unterstützung ebenso zu großem Dank verpflichtet wie dem Hatje Cantz Verlag, der uns bei der Herausgabe des umfangreichen Werkkatalogs unterstützt hat, sowie allen Leihgebern, die die Ausstellungen mit wichtigen Exponaten bereichert haben.

Stephan Berg, Kunstverein Hannover
Ellen Seifermann, Kunsthalle Nürnberg
Els Barents, Huis Marseille, Stiftung für Fotografie, Amsterdam

Down to the Waterline

Stephan Berg

One sees a sea of buildings—the totality of an urban context that has apparently lost all traces of individuality. Thrown together in a chaos of anonymous high-rise structures, structured only by a few lines that cut like canyons through its mass, the city appears as a ceaselessly growing organism that, heedless of humanity, is governed only by its own logic. *Untitled* (1989–97) comprises a forty-eight-part tableau of Tokyo created by Naoya Hatakeyama over a period of nine years. The artist's gaze upon the city of ten million appears initially as cool and detached as the mechanics of his apparatus itself. Everything indicative of development, narration, or a hierarchical relationship among the different parts of the picture has been rigorously eliminated. The bird's-eye perspective used by the artist in each of the individual photographs suggests a panoramic overview that is revealed as its precise opposite in light of the photographic reality. Forty-eight times, the city appears as a pure surface structure, a tectonic texture that has no beginning and no end and thus also lacks a horizon against which it might be differentiated. "There used to be civilization on this planet," writes Hatakeyama in one of the texts that regularly accompany his photographic investigations. "One day, however, the people who created this civilization completely vanished."[1]

This statement reveals much about the attitude that shapes the specific atmosphere of this series and other works by the Japanese artist. The first aspect worth noting here is that of remoteness, an unbridgeable distance to things that are in a certain sense photographed as if he who made them had never been involved in the events he records. A related aspect is the principle of deletion—the encircling of an empty center. Because Hatakeyama's photos focus on structures created by human beings, but never show people, all of his pictures have the look of reconstructions, representations of an alien world that is empty (and devoid of meaning), a world at which we gaze as if looking at the remains of an ancient culture at an archaeological excavation site. In a third, and perhaps most important sense, however, Hatakeyama's photographs are meditations on the suspension of time. The *Untitled* series covers a period of nine years, but there is no recognizable difference between the first and the last images of the tableau. Naturally, the city appears literally in a different, sometimes magical light in the rhythm of day and night, but no pattern of continuous development is evident in these changes. The images form an overview that has no temporal progression and thus no before or after, suggesting instead only a remarkable insistence upon the permanence of the momentary that always appears equal yet somehow different. In the *Blast* series, which has been in progress since 1995, Hatakeyama has found an equally suggestive and precise mode of visual articulation for this coincidence of the eternal and the momentary. In his medium-sized horizontal formats, we witness detonations in several different limestone quarries at the exact moment they occur: the explosive, dynamic force of clouds of stone whirling through the air, frozen in a perpetual still image that transforms the mundane process of quarrying limestone into a sculptural event that is sufficient unto itself in its horrifying beauty and futility.

David Lynch's *Wild at Heart*, a film made in 1990, opens with a completely dark screen. Then a match bursts aflame in this total blackness, filling the entire frame with fiery light, a crackling, greedy blaze that seems to consume not only itself but also the celluloid on which it was captured. The two visual worlds converge for a moment in this paradoxical, iconoclastic structure, for one could easily read the detonation image in Naoya Hatakeyama's *Blast* as a reference to the explosion of the photograph, to its atomization into thousands of tiny fragments, and thus to its potential annihilation.

Yet the central focus of this photographic series is the dramatic, theatrical visualization of a moment that, quite significantly, is not perceptible to our eye but only to the lens of a high-speed, remote-controlled camera.

In order to comprehend the significance of this moment, it is necessary to look back at the first major series done by the Japanese artist, his *Lime Hills (Quarry Series)* of 1986 to 1991 and the *Lime Works (Factory Series)* of 1991 to 1994: an extensive sequence of small color photographs of limestone quarries and associated factories. The factories appear as complex, almost archaic-looking conglomerations of machinery, always devoid of people and usually presented as frame-filling images. Under the gaze of Hatakeyama's camera, the limestone quarries become surreal wastelands. We see white-powdered piles of stone, brownish-orange cuts in green hillside forests that look like gigantic bite marks, and a chaotic array of rocks in the golden, warm evening light. A barren, brownish-white terraced plain in the background, with a red flag stuck in the ground on its forward edge, evokes the impression of a distant planet on which astronauts have placed the flag as a symbol of conquest.

The images Hatakeyama creates in these series are both magical and cold. Their gaze is focused on the seam between nature and technology, but they show no trace of sentimental empathy with nature. In a way, the burgeoning, organoid structures of the factories evoke a stronger sense of nature than the stockpiles of stone and the quarries, in which landscape and nature appear only as voids, as stages in a process of atrophy. On the other hand, nothing could be further from Hatakeyama's intent than a gratuitous critique of civilization that decries the crude exploitation of nature in the documentation of these quarries. The idea of preserving a kind of precivilized natural paradise in the midst of our high-tech reality is exposed for what it really is in these photos: a helpless attempt to domesticate nature as nature parks. In a lecture on his art, Hatakeyama once offered a sarcastic anecdote in reference to this theme: in response to the expression of concern for the "poor mountains" by a member of the Emperor's family in Japan, the mining company immediately painted the open, wounded mountain flanks with green paint, thereby restoring the original intact character of the landscape, at least for those looking upon it from a distance.[2]

Nature, in Hatakeyama's view, is a whole that is subject to all of the developments of our world. There is no antagonism toward the mechanisms of civilization; indeed, nature is a necessary precondition for them. This line of thinking does not imply the end of nature, of course, but only its continuous metamorphosis and transformation. And it is for that very reason that limestone has played a prominent role as a theme and motif in Hatakeyama's artistic concept. This geological rock represents a natural substance which—as an essential component of cement, but also of paper, medicines, and foodstuffs—becomes a pivotal point of intersection between nature and technological progress.[3]

Viewed from this perspective, Hatakeyama's *Blasts* are more than mere visualizations of a dramatic collision between the slow process of the formation of geologic rock over thousands of years and its shockingly sudden destruction. The moment of detonation, which is a prerequisite for the later use of the limestone in cement, for example, becomes the moment in which the nature of stone and the nature of the city converge. Flying into Tokyo, Hatakeyama experienced the city as a mirror-image, a counterpart of the quarries he had just left behind: "The uneven white scene spreading endlessly was not the limestone I had seen in the mine, but the buildings of the city of Tokyo. It suddenly appeared to me that the minerals in the huge emptiness had not simply disappeared but were carried all the way here to be transformed and exist right in front of me."[4] The mirror-image correspondence of these two situations becomes even stronger with the realization that the deep holes left by the quarries in the earth's crust represent, so to speak, the negative volume of what is built up by cities elsewhere. Structurally speaking, one could argue that the positive aspect of the city requires the negative quality, the gap, at a different place in order to become visible. At the same time, this void is also—in a metaphorical sense—the place at which the city will submerge again at some distance time in the future.

The link between excavation and the building of layers serves as a reference to an archeological, vertical principle to which Hatakeyama devoted considerable attention even before he began work on the *Blast* series. If we see the city as a structure consisting of all of the layers stripped from the quarry, it becomes interpretable as a kind of paradoxical archaeological texture. It is precisely this texture that Hatakeyama has pursued in his photographic series since 1993. The *River Series* of 1993–94 and *Underground* of 1999 represent the logical extension of what had begun in the *Untitled* series. Working from the bird's-eye view, in which the city appears as a totality subject to its own laws, the camera descends step by step into the depths of the vertical canyons of the metropolis. In *River Series,* we see canals running through the city in the lower portions of the photographs—like an ironic reminder of a completely regulated, domesticated nature. In the upper halves of the photos, the city appears as an anonymous, strictly vertical accumulation of high-rise architectures accompanied by either a daytime or a nighttime sky. What is important in these photographs, however, is not only the dialectical juxtaposition of nature and architecture in keeping with the pattern of argumentation described above, but above all the manner of staging they exhibit, which clearly shows the extent to which Hatakeyama's images are always self-reflections of the medium of photography. Positioning his camera at an elevated point above the middle of the riverbed, he effectively divides each photograph into two seemingly separate zones of nearly identical size. The edges of the concrete riverbanks form the horizontal line along which the photos appears to split into an upper and a lower half. But there is more involved here than a simple *trompe-l'œil* effect, the ultimate exposure of a supposedly digital or collage process as the perfect craft of the master. And the reference to the capacity of the medium to present the whole as separate parts, and in the act of closer investigation to put them back together to form a much more complex whole, does not exhaust the full range of meaning encompassed by this series of images. Also of crucial importance is the horizontal line along which the upper zone of the photograph is literally mirrored in the lower, as an aesthetic principle, a metaphorical artist's credo.

As structure, the horizontal line is present in the serial concept underlying all of Hatakeyama's works, and it also points here in a paradoxical form to the aspect of time in these works—paradoxical because, as shown above with reference to *Untitled,* time is not conceived primarily as a linear aspect in Hatakeyama's art but instead as a curiously vibrant state of suspension in which the momentary and the eternal converge. In the *River Series,* the horizontal line also represents Hatakeyama's attempt to escape the "terror" of perspective: "Although perspective, now in a state of virtual ruin, has thus far dominated the world of photography, it is this horizontal line that escapes its spells and breaks free."[5] The photos in this series actually do adhere to this principle in that they return the lines of the concrete banks that vanish in perspective to a strictly horizontal plane and thus integrate depth of field into the flat surface. The flattening of space through line heightens the stage-like or set-like effect that plays such an important part in nearly all of Hatakeyama's works. Taken to its ultimate logical consequence, the absolute priority of line would be achieved in the merger of the upper and lower zones of the photograph with it. It is this phantasm Hatakeyama professes to seek when he says, "I think fondly of this line and try to place myself upon it. However, a line has no space. Just as I am on the line, I realize that it occupies no space and, as though I were being swallowed up by it, I vanish too. Just like the people of the former civilization."[6]

Viewed from this angle, the consistent absence of people in all of his works assumes a dynamic quality that flows over to the author of the photographs. The Japanese artist himself is affected by the strange ambivalence of absence and presence, of structure and void, that is evident in all of his photographic series. This interplay of emptiness and substance is perhaps most readily perceptible in *Underground,* in which Hatakeyama leads us literally into the depths of the city. The nether realm of the sewers is ruled by total darkness, and it reminds the photographer that this "underworld" does not need him at all: "Of all the things in the sheer darkness, nothing needs light except me. Here is a world which can exist with or without light. I am the alien, wanting something that is not there."[7] In this situation, the photo series becomes a dual quest for light as the fundamental prerequisite for our ability to see and at the same time as the precondition for the photographic process.[8] A source of light placed in most cases on a tripod in the middle of the frame of view not only illuminates the canals, turning them into scenes that call to mind both caves and stages or occasionally the shutter of the camera, but also consistently transforms the sequence–as in the *River Series*–into a series of investigations into the conditions affecting the photographic image.

In a detail view of the noxiously shimmering surfaces of the waste water in *Underground/Water* and its foamy sediments, Hatakeyama then not only exposes the bizarre, surreal beauty that lies hidden—ordinarily in darkness—in the detritus of our urban societies, but also permits us to draw parallels between this perspective and the panoramic views of Tokyo. In a certain sense, the macroscopic view of the seemingly autonomous growth of the city is repeated in the microscopic perspective of the sewer landscapes, which have the look of unexplored continents on which new worlds could emerge.

This view of our world—both detached and eagerly curious as it is—is evident again in Hatakeyama's two most recent series, *Slow Glass* and *Still Life* (2001). In both of these works, Hatakeyama enters new terrain in departing for the first time ever from Japan and Tokyo as the setting and place of reference for his photographs. In terms of theme, however, we find links to the artist's earlier works in both of these series done during a studio fellowship in the English town of Milton Keynes between April and August 2001. *Slow Glass* presents vague, blurred views of Milton Keynes, ostensibly photographed through windshields covered with drops of rain. What may seem banal at first turns out upon closer examination to be a complex investigation of the relationships between presentation and representation.

We see not only raindrops on a windshield, which puts us in the driver's position, but also everything that is captured in each one of them, as in a small lens. Not only does each raindrop reflect the reality outside the window—which because of the raindrops and the camera's sharp focus on them is perceptible only as a vague blur—it is also a reflection of the mechanics of the camera lens that is focused on it. Thus we see the eye of the camera observing itself in its view of the raindrops. And we also see how the possibility of perceiving reality is diminished by the multiple refractions of view, beginning with the camera and proceeding through the raindrops to the windshield and the reality that lies behind it, to the extent that it becomes fixed in the "closed circuit" of a self-referential perception.

Still Life also works with an apparently artificial view. Here, Hatakeyama presents images of a housing development in Milton Keynes—most of them bathed in warm light—as a strangely surreal model settlement. Standardized row houses, perfectly straight sidewalks, and freshly paved streets are embedded in grass-green landscapes that look quite as unreal as the houses themselves. The development could serve as a perfect blueprint for a sequel to Peter Weir's 1998 movie *The Truman Show*, yet it also evokes the impression that shooting had not yet begun or had long since come to an end. This is due not only to Hatakeyama's specific photographic approach but also to the fact that the entire town actually was created more or less as an idealized drawing-board model based upon plans drafted by the American city planner Melvin Webber. Of course, this series is also a commentary on the typical products of standardized British building policy, just as *Untitled* is a reflection on unfettered Japanese urbanism. Above all, however, it is further evidence of Hatakeyama's ability to generate images in which the self-reflective nature of the photographic process converges with the visualization of a world full of equally suggestive and untouchable surfaces, a world frozen in an eternal moment.

1 Naoya Hatakeyama, "River Series," in *Lust und Leere: Japanische Photographie*, edited by Peter Weiermair and Gerald Matt, Zurich 1997, p. 33.

2 Naoya Hatakeyama, quoted from an unpublished lecture delivered during the "Study Day" at the Victoria and Albert Museum in London on November 9, 2001. The lecture was presented in conjunction with the exhibition entitled *Out of Japan* (Felice Beato, Masahisa Fukase, Naoya Hatakeyama).

3 Limestone is the only raw material available in such abundance in Japan that the country is able to supply its own demand.

4 Hatakeyama 2001 (see footnote 2).

5 Hatakeyama 1997 (see footnote 1), p. 33.

6 Ibid.

7 Naoya Hatakeyama, *Underground*, Tokyo 2000, p. 4.

8 The significance of light in Hatakeyama's art is also made evident in the 1996 series entitled *Maquettes/Light*. The series contains images of extremely flat light boxes with black-and-white prints of nightlights in stairways or outdoor areas around apartment buildings. The photographed light blends with the invisible light of the light boxes, creating a disturbing effect that is not only intended to liberate light from its metaphorical meaning and expose it at the level of the physical (Hatakeyama) but also plays upon the structural ambivalence between description and the described and the yearning of photography not only to touch its motifs physically—in the sense of an index trace—but also to embody them in a literal sense.

Down to the Waterline

Stephan Berg

Zu sehen ist ein Häusermeer. Die Totalität eines urbanen Zusammenhangs, dem scheinbar jedes individuelle Moment abhanden gekommen ist. Chaotisch durcheinander gewürfelt aus anonymen Hochhausstrukturen, gegliedert allein durch einige schluchtartige Schneisen, zeigt sich die Stadt als wuchernder Organismus, der anscheinend ohne jede Rücksicht auf den Menschen allein seiner eigenen Logik gehorcht. *Untitled* (1989–1997) umfasst ein 48-teiliges Tableau, das Naoya Hatakeyama über einen neunjährigen Zeitraum von Tokio erstellt hat. Der Blick, den der Künstler auf die Zehnmillionenstadt wirft, wirkt zunächst so kühl und desinteressiert wie die Mechanik der Apparatur selbst, die er benutzt. Konsequent wird alles ausgeblendet, woraus sich Entwicklung, Narration oder ein hierarchischer Zusammenhang der einzelnen Bildteile herleiten ließe. Die Vogelperspektive, die der Künstler in jedem der einzelnen Bildtafeln einnimmt, suggeriert eine Übersicht, die sich angesichts der Bildrealität in ihr Gegenteil verkehrt. 48-mal erscheint die Stadt als eine reine Oberflächenstruktur, als eine tektonische Textur, die keinen Anfang und kein Ende kennt und infolgedessen auch keinen Horizont, gegen den sie differenziert werden könnte. »There used to be civilization on this planet«, schreibt Hatakeyama in einem der Texte, die seine fotografischen Investigationen regelmäßig begleiten, »one day, however, the people who created this civilization completely vanished.«[1]

In diesem Satz steckt ein Großteil der Haltung, die die spezifische Atmosphäre nicht nur dieser Serie des Japaners bestimmt. Zuerst ist hier das Moment der Ferne zu nennen, die unaufhebbare Distanz zu den Dingen, die in gewisser Weise so fotografiert werden, als wäre derjenige, der sie gemacht hat, an dem Geschehen, das er aufzeichnet, nie beteiligt gewesen. Dazu kommt als verwandter Aspekt das Prinzip der Aussparung: das Umkreisen eines leeren Zentrums. Da Hatakeyamas Fotos sich mit Strukturen beschäftigen, die von Menschen erzeugt wurden, ohne diese dabei je zu zeigen, erscheinen im Ergebnis alle Bilder des Künstlers als Rekonstruktionen, die eine fremde, (sinn)leere Welt vergegenwärtigen, auf die wir wie auf eine archäologische Ausgrabungsstätte aus fernen Zeiten blicken. In dritter und vielleicht wichtigster Hinsicht aber sind Hatakeyamas Fotografien Meditationen über eine zum Stillstand gekommene Zeit. Neun Jahre umfasst die Serie *Untitled*, aber zwischen dem ersten und dem letzten Bild des Tableaus gibt es keinen entscheidenden Unterschied. Wohl zeigt sich die Stadt im Rhythmus von Tag und Nacht jedes Mal buchstäblich in einem anderen, bisweilen magischen Licht, aber eine fortschreitende Entwicklung lässt sich daraus nicht ablesen. Die Bilder formieren sich zu einem Überblick, der keine zeitliche Sukzession und damit auch kein Vorher oder Später kennt, sondern nur ein eigentümliches Insistieren auf einer Permanenz des Augen-Blicklichen, das immer gleich und doch immer anders erscheint.

In der seit 1995 entstehenden Serie der *Blast* findet Naoya Hatakeyama für diese Koinzidenz aus Ewigkeit und Moment eine ebenso suggestive wie präzise Bildformulierung. Auf horizontalen, mittelgroßen Formaten sehen wir in verschiedenen Kalksteinbrüchen exakt den Moment der Sprengung: die explosive, dynamische Kraft der durch die Luft wirbelnden Steinwolken, eingefroren auf ein ewiges Standbild, das den profanen Akt des Abbaus von Kalkstein in ein skulpturales Ereignis verwandelt, welches schrecklich-schön und zwecklos sich selbst genügt.

In David Lynchs Film *Wild at Heart* aus dem Jahr 1990 ist die Leinwand zunächst völlig dunkel. Dann flammt in dieser totalen Schwärze ein Streichholz auf und erfüllt das gesamte Bild mit seinem feurigen Schein, einem knisternden gierigen Brennen, das nicht nur sich selbst zu verzehren scheint, sondern auch das Zelluloid, auf das es gebannt wurde. In dieser paradox ikonoklastischen Struktur berühren sich beide Bildwelten für einen kurzen Augenblick, denn auch in den *Blast* von Naoya Hatakeyama könnte man die Repräsentation des Sprengakts als einen metaphorischen Hinweis auf die Explosion des Bildes lesen, auf seine Atomisierung in Tausende von kleinen Fragmenten und damit seine mögliche Auslöschung.

Der zentrale Fokus dieser Bildreihe aber liegt auf der dramatisch-theatralischen Visualisierung eines Augenblicks, der signifikanterweise für unsere Augen nicht erfassbar ist, sondern allein für das Objektiv einer Hochgeschwindigkeitskamera, die mit einer Fernbedienung gesteuert wird.

Um die Bedeutung dieses Augenblicks zu verstehen, muss man auf die ersten großen Serien des Japaners, die *Lime Hills (Quarry Series)* von 1986 bis 1991 und die *Lime Works (Factory Series)* von 1991 bis 1994, zurückkommen, eine umfangreiche Folge kleinformatiger Farbfotografien von Kalksteinbrüchen und den dazugehörigen Fabriken. Die Fabriken erscheinen als komplexe, fast archaisch wirkende Maschinerien, stets völlig menschenleer und meist formatfüllend in den Bildraum platziert. Die Kalksteinbrüche werden unter dem Blick von Hatakeyamas Kamera zu surreal wirkenden Wastelands. Wir sehen weiß gepuderte Halden, orangebräunliche Breschen in grünen Waldhängen, wie gigantische Bissspuren, und chaotisch anmutendes Felsengewirr im goldenen warmen Abendlicht. Eine kahle bräunlichweiße Ebene mit Terrassierungen im Hintergrund, an deren vorderen Rand eine rote Fahne in den Boden gerammt wurde, wirkt wie ein Bild von einem fernen Planeten, auf dem Raumfahrer die Flagge als Zeichen symbolischer Inbesitznahme hinterlasssen haben.

Die Bilder, die Hatakeyama hier entwirft, sind magisch und kalt zugleich. Ihr Blick richtet sich auf die Nahtstelle zwischen Natur und Technik, aber gänzlich ohne sentimentale Naturempathie. Die wuchernd organoiden Strukturen der Fabriken strahlen in gewisser Weise etwas Naturhafteres aus als die Abraumhalden und Steinbrüche, in denen Landschaft und Natur nurmehr als Leerstelle, als Schwundstufe zu besichtigen sind. Andererseits liegt Hatakeyama nichts ferner als eine wohlfeile Zivilisationskritik, die mit der Dokumentation der Steinbrüche die krude Ausbeutung der Natur anprangert. Die Idee der Bewahrung einer sozusagen vorzivilisatorischen Naturidylle inmitten unserer hoch technisierten Wirklichkeit wird in diesen Fotos als das kenntlich gemacht, was sie ist: ein hilfloser Versuch, Natur als Naturparks zu domestizieren. In einem Vortrag zu seiner Arbeit hat Hatakeyama eine sarkastische Anekdote zu diesem Thema beigesteuert: Nachdem sich ein Mitglied der kaiserlichen Familie in Japan Sorgen um die »armen Berge« gemacht hatte, reagierte die Bergbaugesellschaft, indem sie die offenen, verletzten Bergflanken kurzerhand mit grüner Farbe übertünchte, um so zumindest für ein distanziertes Auge die ursprüngliche Homogenität der Landschaft wiederherzustellen.[2]

Natur im Sinne Hatakeyamas ist eine Totalität, der sämtliche Entwicklungen in unserer Welt unterworfen sind: kein Antagonismus zu zivilisatorischen Mechanismen, sondern notwendige Vorbedingung. In diesem Denken gibt es natürlicherweise kein Ende des Naturhaften, sondern nur seine permanente Metamorphose und Transfomation. Eben deshalb wird Kalkstein über viele Jahre zum bestimmenden Thema und Motiv im künstlerischen Denken Hatakeyamas. Das geologische Gestein repräsentiert einen Naturstoff, der – als wichtiger Bestandteil von Zement, aber auch von Papier, Medikamenten und Lebensmitteln – gleichzeitig zur Gelenkstelle zwischen Natur und technologischem Fortschritt wird.[3]

So gesehen, sind die *Blast* nicht nur Visualisierungen eines dramatischen Zusammenpralls zwischen der Langsamkeit jahrtausendealter geologischer Gesteinsbildung und ihrer schockhaft plötzlichen Zerstörung. Der Moment der Sprengung, der ja die Vorbedingung ist für die spätere Verwendung des Kalksteins beispielsweise im Zement, wird zum Augenblick, an dem sich die Natur des Steins mit der Natur der Stadt kurzschließt. Bei einem Anflug auf Tokio erlebt Hatakeyama die Stadt als spiegelbildliches Gegenstück zu den Steinbrüchen, die er gerade verlassen hatte: »The uneven white scene spreading endlessly was not the limestone I had seen in the mine, but the buildings of the city of Tokyo. It suddenly appeared to me that the minerals in the huge emptiness had not simply disappeared but were carried all the way here to be transformed and exist right in front of me.«[4] Die Spiegelbildlichkeit beider Situationen verstärkt sich noch, sobald man sich klar macht, dass die tiefen Löcher, die die Steinbrüche in der Erdkruste hinterlassen, sozusagen das Negativvolumen dessen darstellen, was durch die Städte an anderer Stelle errichtet wird. Strukturell gesehen, ließe sich also argumentieren, dass das Positiv der Stadt, um sichtbar zu werden, das Negativ, die Lücke an anderer Stelle benötigt. Gleichzeitig ist diese Leerstelle aber auch – metaphorisch gesehen – der Ort, in den die Stadt in irgendeiner fernen Zukunft wieder zurücksinken wird.

Die Verknüpfung von Aushub und Schichtung weist dabei auf ein archäologisches, vertikales Prinzip hin, dem sich Hatakeyama schon vor der Serie der *Blast* verstärkt gewidmet hat. Begreift man die Stadt als eine Struktur, die vor allem aus den abgetragenen Schichten der Steinbrüche besteht, wird sie lesbar als eine Art paradoxer archäologischer Textur. Eben dieser Textur folgt Hatakeyama in seinen fotografischen Serien seit 1993. Die *River Series* von 1993/94 und *Underground* von 1999 sind dabei die konsequente Fortsetzung dessen, was mit der Serie *Untitled* begonnen wurde: Ausgehend von der Vogelperspektive, aus der sich die Stadt als eine Totalität mit ganz eigenen Gesetzen zeigt, arbeitet sich die Kamera nun Stück für Stück in die Tiefen der vertikalen Schluchten der Metropole vor. In den *River Series* sehen wir auf der unteren Bildhälfte – wie eine ironische Erinnerung an eine vollkommen regulierte, domestizierte Natur – Kanäle, die die Stadt durchziehen; auf der oberen Bildhälfte erscheint die Stadt als anonyme, strikt vertikal bestimmte Hochhausarchitektur, zu der jeweils ein tagheller oder nächtlicher Himmelsausschnitt tritt. Wichtig ist in diesen Aufnahmen aber nicht nur die dialektische Verklammerung von Natur und Architektur, die dem oben beschriebenen Argumentationsmuster folgt, sondern vor allem die Art der Inszenierung, die deutlich macht, wie sehr Hatakeyamas Bilder immer auch Selbstreflexionen des fotografischen Mediums sind. Indem der Künstler seine Kamera jeweils erhöht mittig im Flussbett positioniert, gelingt es ihm, das Bild in zwei scheinbar komplett getrennte, fast identisch große Bildzonen zu zerlegen. Die Ränder der betonierten Flussufer bilden dabei die horizontale Linie, an der das Foto in einen oberen und einen unteren Teil zu zerfallen scheint. Dahinter steckt mehr, als das schlichte Trompe-l'Œil, ein vermeintlich digitales oder collagierendes Verfahren schlussendlich als perfekt beherrschtes Handwerk zu enttarnen. Und auch der Hinweis auf die Macht des Mediums, uns das Zusammengehörige als Getrenntes vorzuführen, das sich im Akt der vertiefenden Betrachtung wieder zu einem nunmehr wesentlich komplexeren Ganzen zusammenfügt, erschöpft nicht den gesamten Bedeutungsgehalt dieser Bildfolge. Von zentraler Bedeutung ist die horizontale Linie, an der sich die obere Bildzone buchstäblich in der unteren spiegelt, vielmehr auch als ästhetisches Prinzip, als metaphorisches künstlerisches Kredo.

Als Struktur ist die horizontale Linie schon in der seriellen Anlage aller Arbeiten Hatakeyamas enthalten und verweist hier in widersprüchlicher Form auf den Zeitaspekt der Arbeiten. Widersprüchlich deshalb, weil, wie bereits bei *Untitled* gezeigt, Zeit bei Hatakeyama nicht primär als lineares Moment der Sukzession gedacht wird, sondern als merkwürdig vibrierender Stillstand, in dem sich Augenblick und Ewigkeit berühren. In den *River Series* ist die horizontale Linie darüber hinaus auch Hatakeyamas Versuch, dem »Terror« der Perspektive zu entkommen: »Although perspective, now in a state of virtual ruin, has thus far dominated the world of photography, it is this horizontal line that escapes its spells and breaks free.«[5] Tatsächlich folgen die Aufnahmen der Serie diesem Prinzip, indem sie die perspektivisch in der Flucht verlaufenden Linien der Betonufer durch die Kameraperspektive strikt horizontalisieren und somit die Bildtiefe in die Fläche zurückbinden. Das Flacherwerden des Raums durch die Linie verstärkt seine Bühnen- und Kulissenhaftigkeit, die in nahezu allen Arbeiten Hatakeyamas eine wichtige Rolle spielt. Konsequent zu Ende gedacht, wäre die absolute Priorität der Linie dann erreicht, wenn die obere und die untere Bildzone mit ihr zusammenfallen würden. Es ist dieses Phantasma, dem Hatakeyama erklärtermaßen folgt, wenn er ausführt: »I think fondly of this line and try to place myself upon it. However, a line has no space. Just as I am on the line, I realize that it occupies no space and, as if I were being swallowed up by it, I vanish too. Just like the people of the former civilization.«[6]

Von dieser Seite aus betrachtet, erhält die konsequente Menschenleere in allen Arbeiten eine Dynamik, die auf den Autor der Aufnahmen übergreift. Auch er ist von der merkwürdigen Ambivalenz aus Abwesenheit und Anwesenheit, aus Struktur und Leere betroffen, die sich durch alle Serien des Japaners zieht. In *Underground*, wo Hatakeyama uns buchstäblich auf den Grund der Stadt führt, ist dieses Verhältnis von Leere und Substanz vielleicht am deutlichsten zu erleben. Dort unten in den Abwasserkanälen herrscht die Art von völliger Dunkelheit, die dem fotografierenden Ich klarmacht, dass diese »Unterwelt« nicht auf ihn angewiesen ist: »Of all the things in the sheer darkness, nothing needs light except me. Here is a world which can exist with or without light. I am the alien, wanting something that is not there.«[7] In dieser Situation wird die Fotofolge zu einer doppelten Recherche nach dem Licht als Grundbedingung unserer Wahrnehmung, das gleichzeitig die Voraussetzung für den fotografischen Prozess bildet.[8] Eine meist mittig in den Bildplan gesetzte Lichtquelle auf einem Stativ erhellt nicht nur die Kanäle zu Szenerien, die ebenso an Höhlen wie an Bühnen oder bisweilen an den Verschluss des Kameraobjektivs erinnern, sondern sie verwandelt die Folge – wie in den *River Series* – immer auch in Investigationen nach den Bedingungen des fotografischen Bildes.

Im Detailblick auf die giftig schillernden Abwasseroberflächen in *Underground/Water* und ihren schaumigen Schlick entdeckt Hatakeyama dann nicht nur die bizarr-surreale Schönheit, die in den Rückständen unserer urbanen Gesellschaften – gewöhnlich lichtlos – schlummert, sondern er erlaubt uns auch, eine Parallele dieses Blicks zu den Panoramaansichten von Tokio zu ziehen. In gewisser Weise wiederholt sich der Makroblick auf die scheinbar selbsttätig wuchernde Struktur der Stadt im Mikroblick auf die Abwasserlandschaften, die wie unentdeckte Kontinente wirken, aus denen neue Welten entstehen könnten.

Dieser Blick auf unsere Welt – distanziert und lustvoll neugierig zugleich – findet sich wieder in den zwei neuesten Werkfolgen *Slow Glass* und *Still Life* von 2001. Mit beiden Arbeiten begibt sich Hatakeyama insoweit auf Neuland, als er sich zum ersten Mal von Japan und Tokio als Bezugsort seiner Fotografien löst. Inhaltlich aber gibt es in beiden Serien, die während eines Atelierstipendiums im englischen Milton Keynes zwischen April und August entstanden, durchaus Verbindungslinien zu den früheren Arbeiten des Künstlers. *Slow Glass* zeigt unbestimmt und verschwommen bleibende Ansichten von Milton Keynes, scheinbar fotografiert durch Windschutzscheiben, die mit Regentropfen bedeckt sind. Was sich im ersten Moment banal anhören mag, entpuppt sich bei genauerer Betrachtung als komplexe Untersuchung der Verhältnisse zwischen Präsentation und Repräsentation.

Wir sehen nämlich nicht nur die Regentropfen auf der Scheibe, die uns in die Perspektive von Autofahrern versetzt, sondern auch das, was in jedem von ihnen, wie in einer kleinen Linse, gespeichert ist. Jeder Regentropfen spiegelt nicht nur die Realität vor dem Fenster – die wir aufgrund der Regentropfen und des Fokus der Kamera, der auf die Tropfen scharf gestellt ist, nur verschwommen erahnen können –, sondern wird auch zur Spiegelung der Mechanik des Kameraobjektivs, das auf sie gerichtet ist. Wir sehen also den Blick der Kamera, der sich im Blick auf die Regentropfen selbst beobachtet. Und wir sehen, wie dabei die Möglichkeit, die Realität wahrzunehmen, durch die mehrfache Brechung des Blicks, angefangen von der Kamera über die Regentropfen bis hin zu der Scheibe und der dahinter liegenden Wirklichkeit, so weit abgebremst wird, bis er am Ende im »closed circuit« einer selbstbezogenen Wahrnehmung stecken bleibt.

Auch *Still Life* operiert mit einem künstlich wirkenden Blick. Zumeist im warmen Licht der Abenddämmerung zeigt uns Hatakeyama ein Wohngebiet in Milton Keynes als merkwürdig surreale Modellsiedlung. Standardisierte Reihenhäuser, schnurgerade Gehwege und frisch asphaltierte Straßen sind eingebettet in grasig grüne Landschaften, die ebenso irreal wirken wie die Häuser selbst. Die Siedlung könnte eine perfekte Blaupause für eine zweite Folge von Peter Weirs *Truman Show* aus dem Jahr 1998 abgeben, aber sie wirkt gleichzeitig so, als hätten die Dreharbeiten noch gar nicht begonnen oder wären längst abgeschlossen. Das liegt nicht nur an der spezifischen fotografischen Annäherung Hatakeyamas, sondern resultiert wesentlich auch aus der Tatsache, dass der gesamte Ort, basierend auf den Entwürfen des amerikanischen Städteplaners Melvin Webber, mehr oder minder als idealisierte Reißbrettsiedlung entstand. Natürlich ist diese Serie auch ein Kommentar auf die typisch standardisierte englische Baupolitik, so wie *Untitled* eine Reflexion über ungebremsten japanischen Urbanismus darstellt. Aber vor allem ist sie ein weiterer Beweis für die Fähigkeit Hatakeyamas, Bilder zu generieren, in denen sich die Selbstreflexion des fotografischen Prozesses mit der Visualisierung einer im ewigen Augenblick eingefrorenen Welt aus lauter ebenso suggestiven wie fremd und unberührbar bleibenden Oberflächen trifft.

1 Naoya Hatakeyama, »River Series«, in: *Lust und Leere. Japanische Photographie*, hrsg. von Peter Weiermair und Gerald Matt, Zürich 1997, S. 33.

2 Naoya Hatakeyama, zit. nach einem unveröffentlichten Vortrag, den er am 9. November 2001 am »Study Day« im Victoria and Albert Museum in London hielt. Der Vortrag begleitete die Ausstellung »Out of Japan« (Felice Beato, Masahisa Fukase, Naoya Hatakeyama).

3 Kalkstein ist der einzige Rohstoff, über den Japan so reichlich verfügt, dass es seinen Bedarf aus eigener Kraft decken kann.

4 Hatakeyama 2001 (wie Anm. 2).

5 Hatakeyama 1997 (wie Anm. 1), S. 33.

6 Ebenda.

7 Naoya Hatakeyama, *Underground*, Tokio 2000, S. 4.

8 Die Bedeutung des Lichts innerhalb des Werks von Hatakeyama wird auch in der 1996 entstandenen Serie *Maquettes/Light* deutlich. Die Folge zeigt extrem flache Lichtboxen mit Schwarzweißprints von Nachtlichtern in Treppenhäusern oder den Außenanlagen von Appartements. Dabei überlagern sich das fotografierte Licht und das reale, aber unsichtbar bleibende Licht der Lichtboxen auf eine irritierende Weise, die nicht nur darauf zielt, Licht von seiner metaphorischen Bedeutung zu befreien und es auf die Ebene des Physischen zu bringen (Hatakeyama), sondern auch mit der strukturellen Ambivalenz zwischen Bezeichnung und Bezeichnetem und der Sehnsucht der Fotografie spielt, ihre Motive nicht nur – im Sinne einer indexalischen Spur – physikalisch zu berühren, sondern diese buchstäblich zu verkörpern.

Lime Works

... When I learned that Japan was a land of limestone, my appreciation of its cityscapes underwent a subtle change. Japan is dependent on imports for most of the minerals it uses, but when it comes to limestone it is totally self-sufficient. Every year some two hundred million tons of limestone are cut from quarries scattered about the country, half being used to make cement and the rest entering our lives in such forms as aggregate for concrete and asphalt, or as iron, glass, paper, ink, plastic, medicines, or foodstuffs.... In the texture of concrete I can feel the trace of corals and fusulinas that inhabited warm equatorial seas two hundred to four hundred million years ago....

If the concrete buildings and highways that stretch to the horizon are all made from limestone dug from the hills, and if they should all be ground to dust and this vast quantity of calcium carbonate returned to its precise points of origin, why then, with the last spoonful, the ridge lines of the hills would be restored to their original dimensions. The quarries and the cities are like negative and positive images of a single photograph....

Lime Works (Factory Series), 1991–94, C-Print, 28.5 x 57.5 cm
Courtesy L.A. Galerie, Frankfurt on Main; the artist

Lime Works

[...] Als ich herausfand, dass Japan ein Kalksteinland ist, hat dies meine Ansicht über die japanischen Städte ein wenig verändert. Bei den meisten Mineralstoffen ist Japan auf Importe angewiesen, doch die Kalksteinvorkommen sind mehr als ausreichend, um den Bedarf zu decken. Jedes Jahr werden in den japanischen Steinbrüchen annähernd zweihundert Millionen Tonnen Kalkstein abgebaut, von denen ungefähr die Hälfte zu Zement verarbeitet wird und der Rest als Bestandteil von Beton und Asphalt oder als Zutat in Eisen, Glas, Papier, Tinte, Arznei- und Lebensmitteln einen Platz in unserem Leben findet. [...] In der Textur des Betons kann ich noch die Spuren von Korallen und Foraminiferen fühlen, die vor zweihundert bis vierhundert Millionen Jahren im warmen äquatorialen Ozean lebten. [...]

Wenn alle aus Beton gebauten Häuser und Straßen, die sich bis an den Horizont erstrecken, aus dem Kalkstein sind, der aus den Bergen gebrochen wurde, und wenn alle diese Häuser und Straßen zu Staub zermahlen würden und diese ungeheure Menge Kalk an ihren genauen Herkunftsort zurückgebracht würde, dann wären mit der letzten Schaufel die Bergkämme in ihren ursprünglichen Dimensionen wiederhergestellt. Die Steinbrüche und die Städte sind wie das Negativ und das Positiv ein und derselben Fotografie. [...]

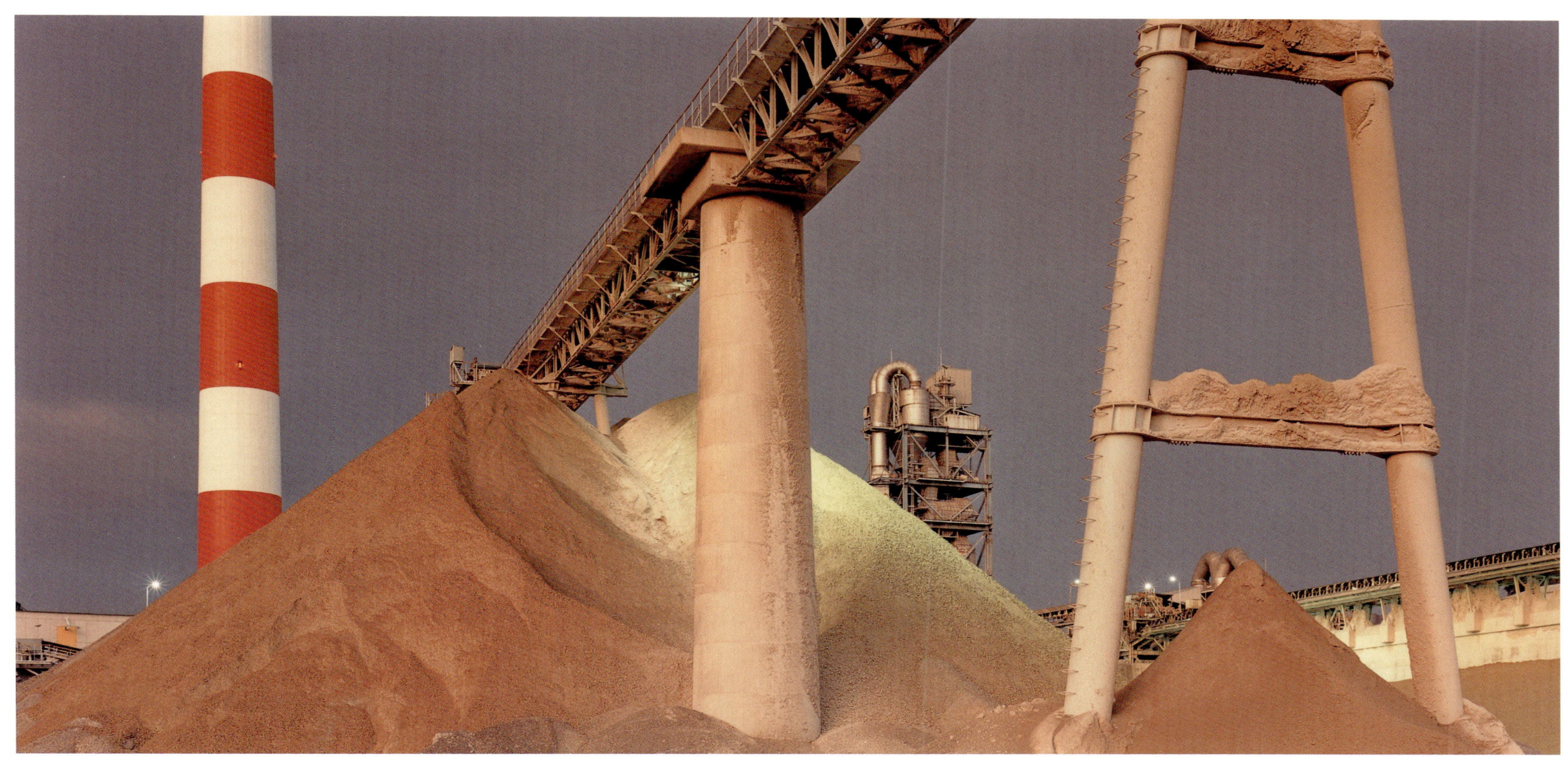

17610

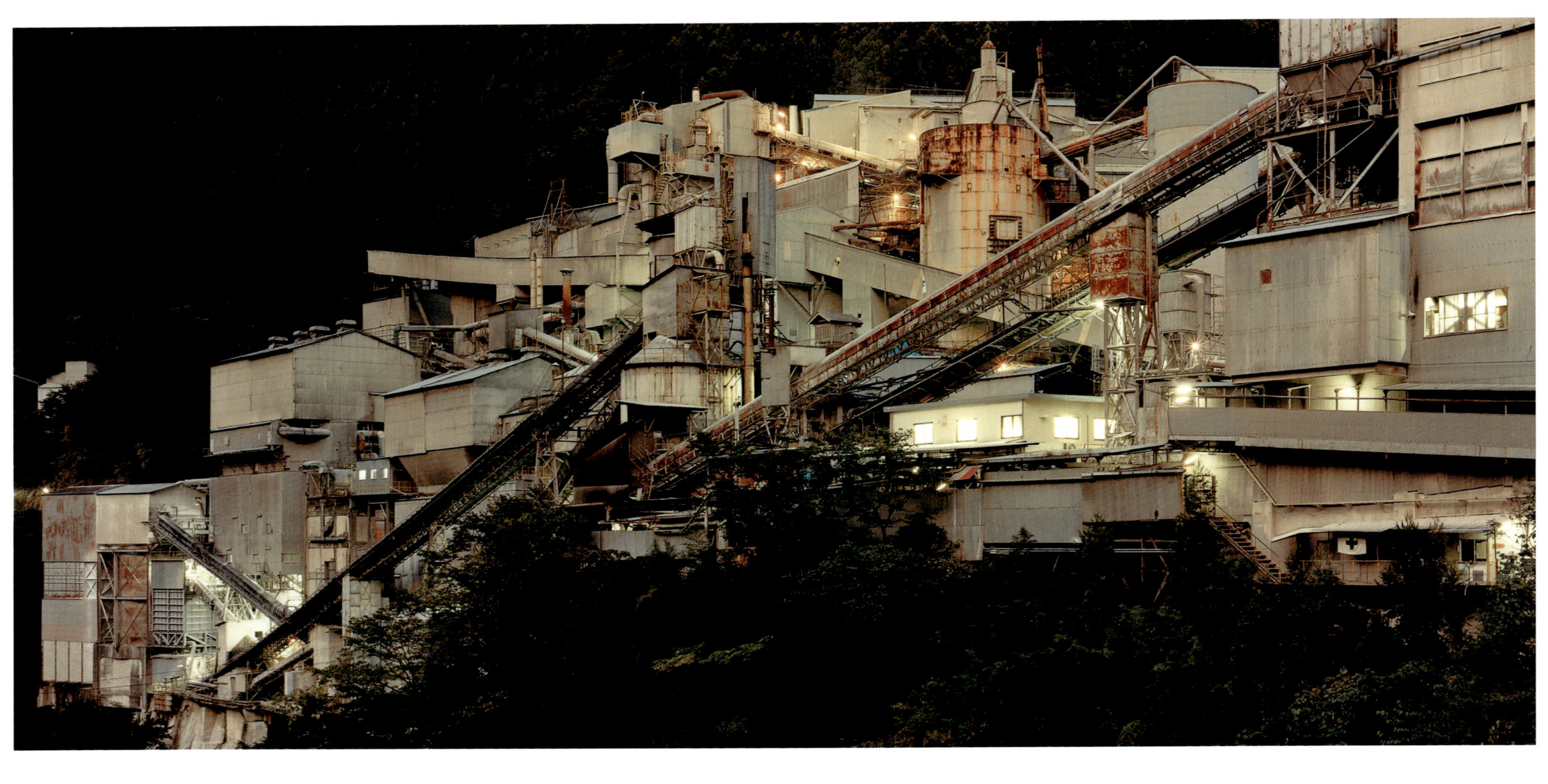

30214

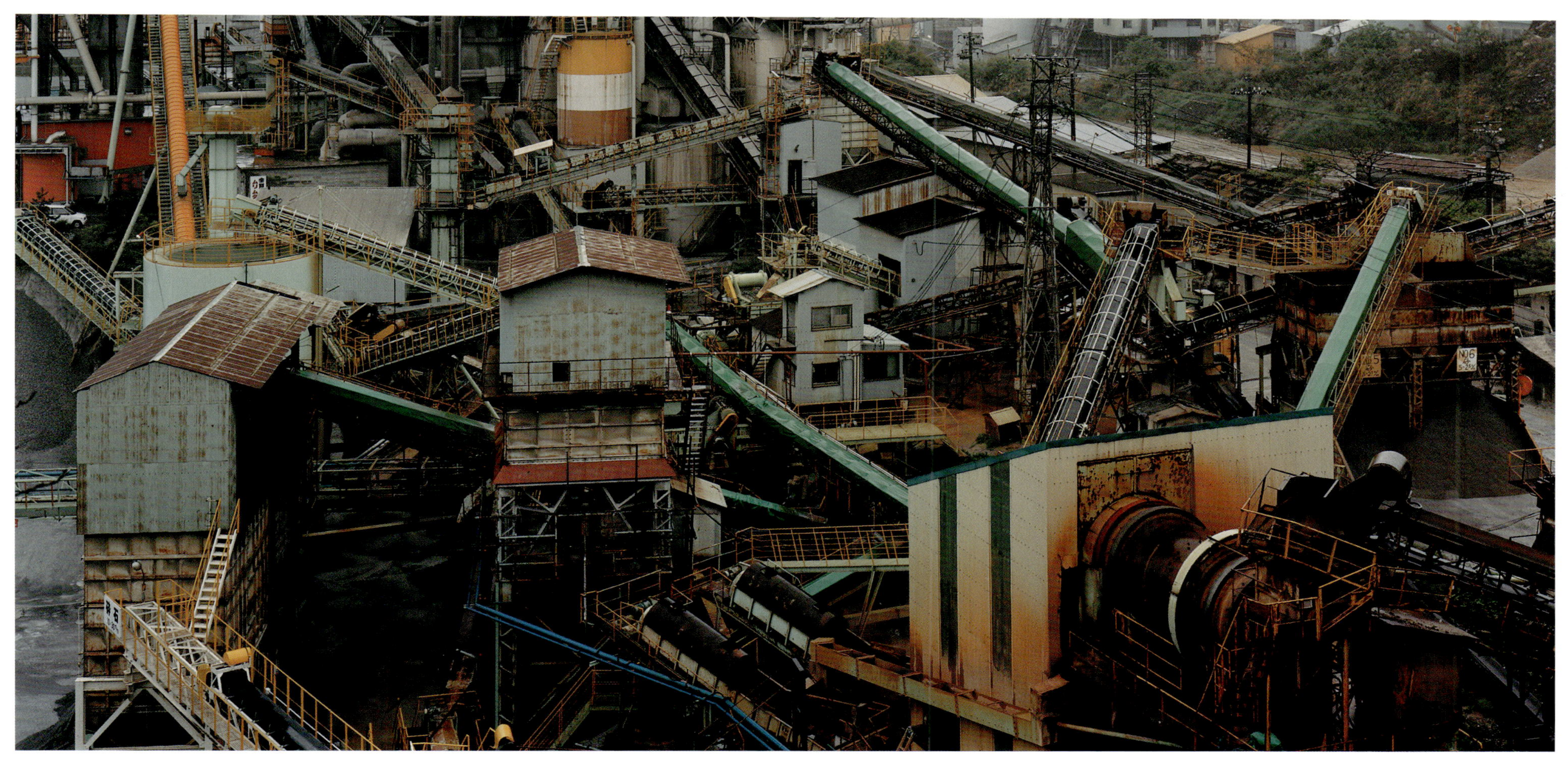

40608

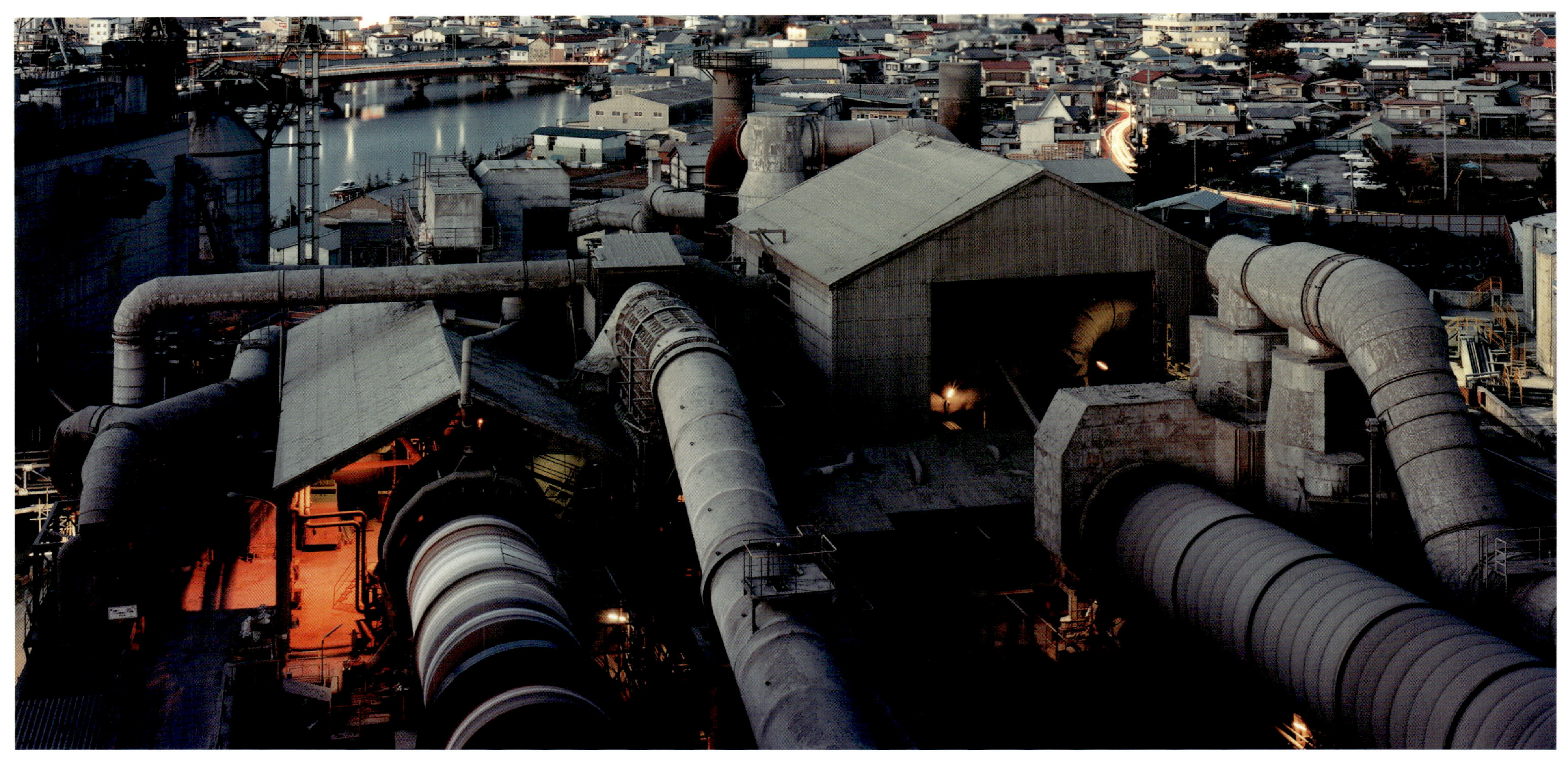

30504

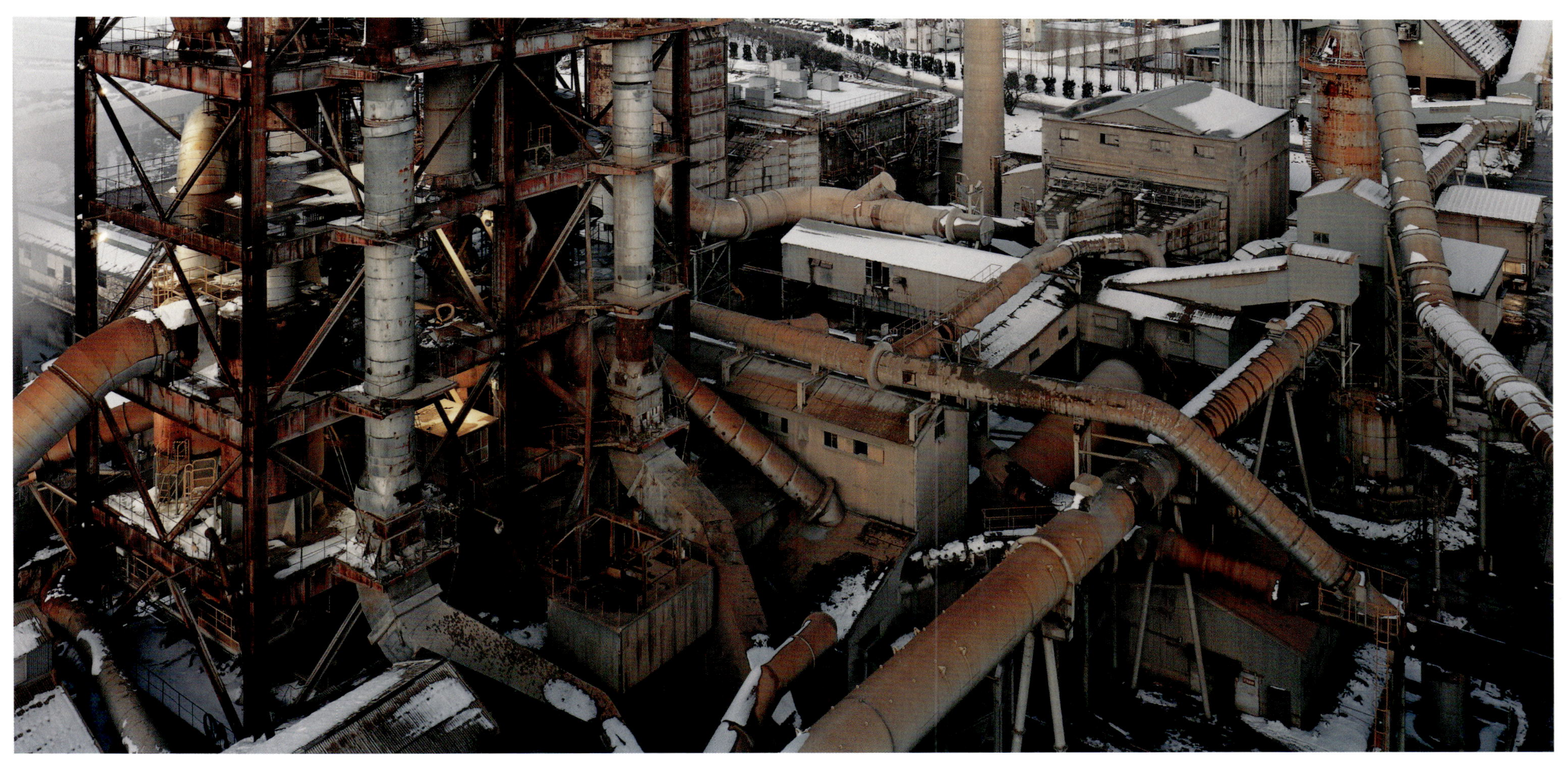

25009

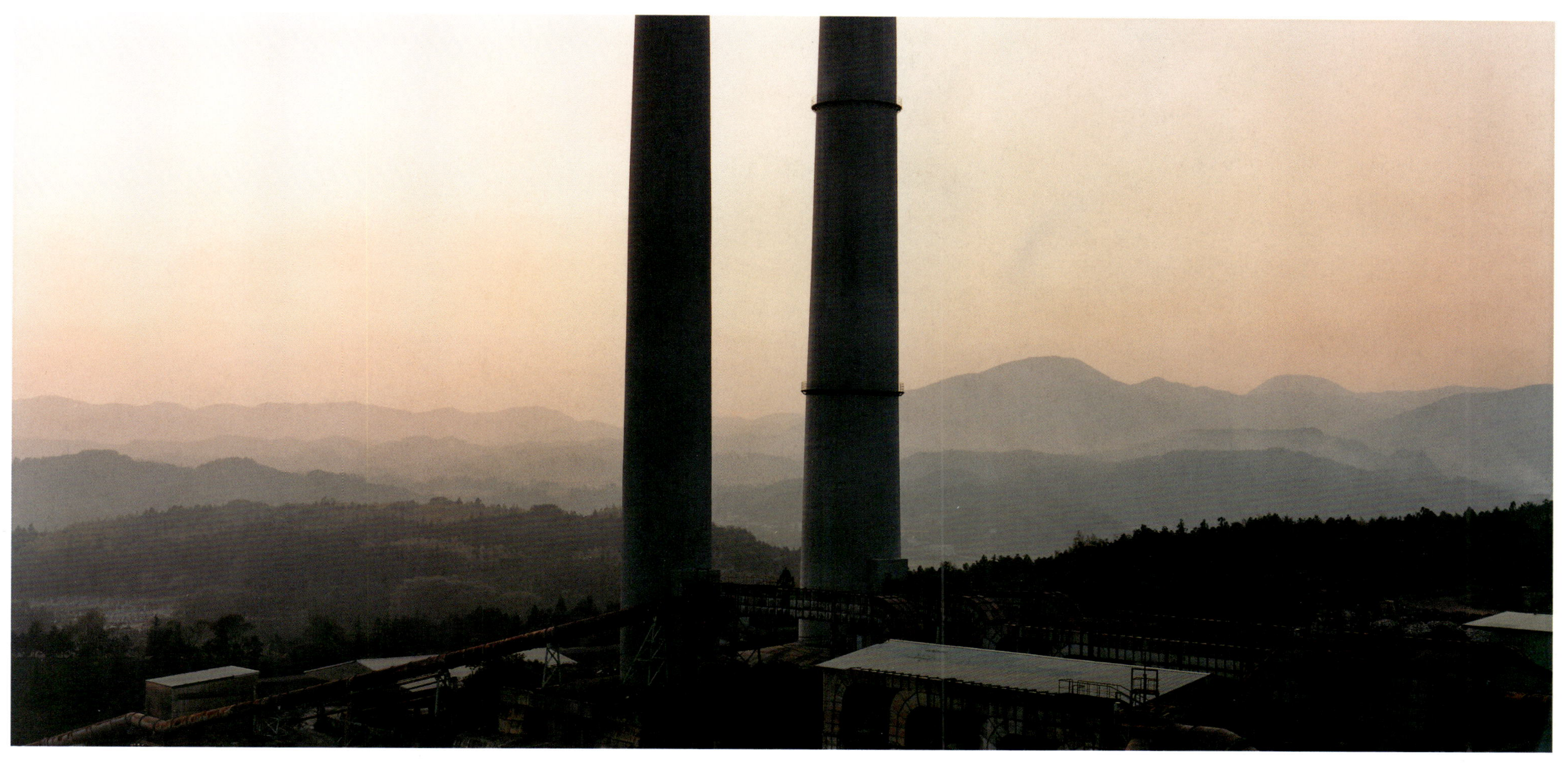

#35414

Lime Hills (Quarry Series)

Lime Hills (Quarry Series), 1986–91, C-Print, 30.8 x 38 cm
Courtesy L.A. Galerie, Frankfurt on Main; the artist

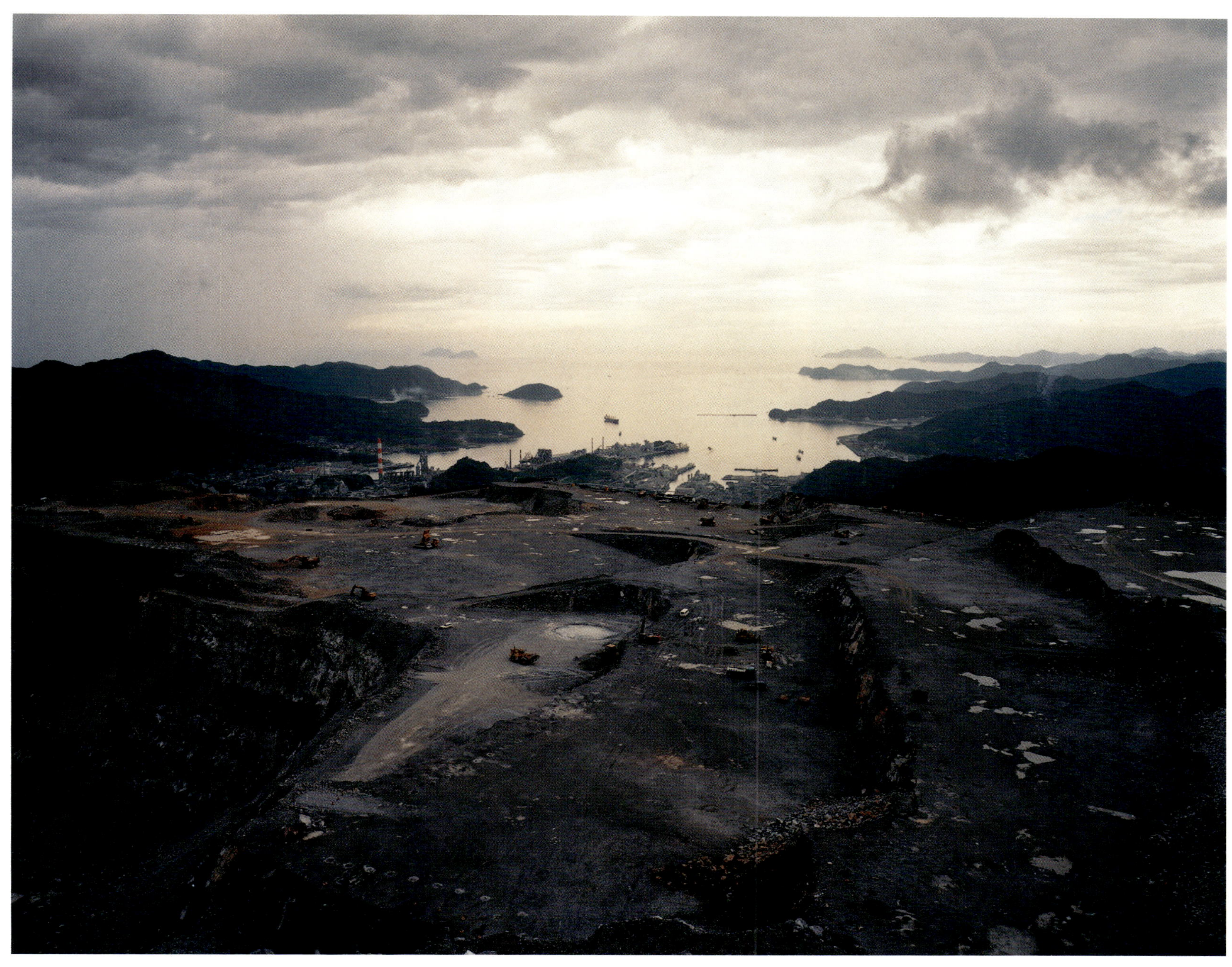

27403

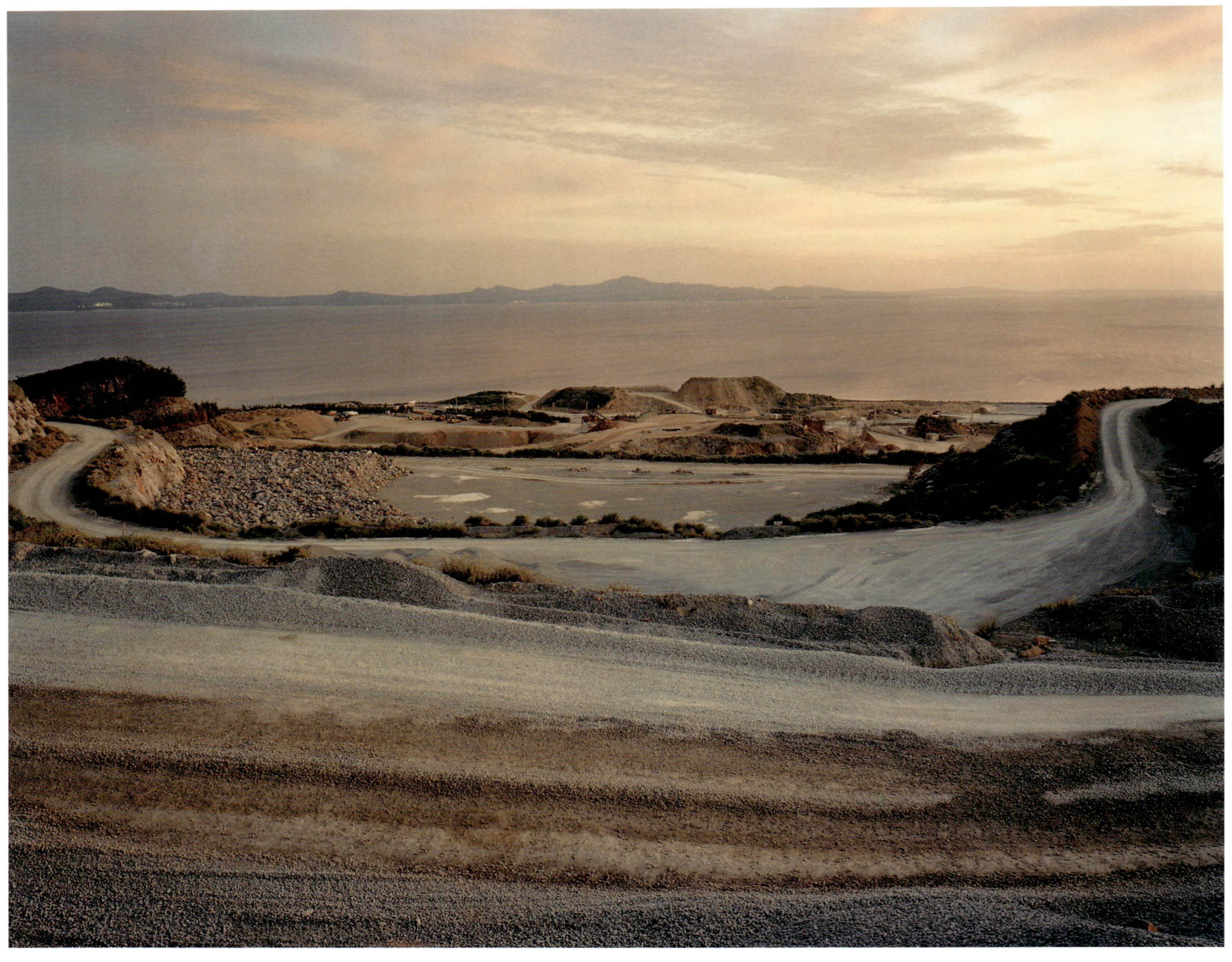

23802

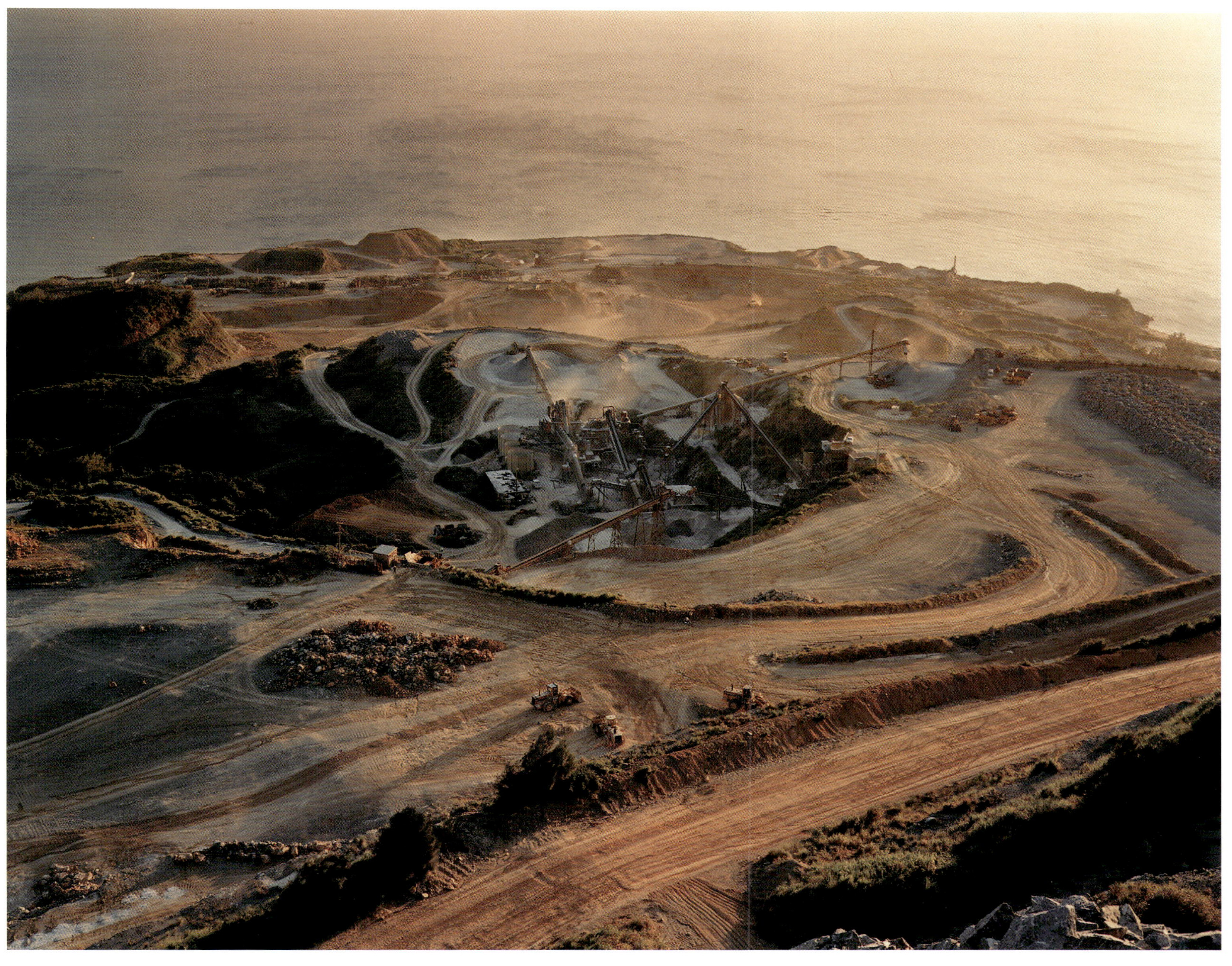

23514

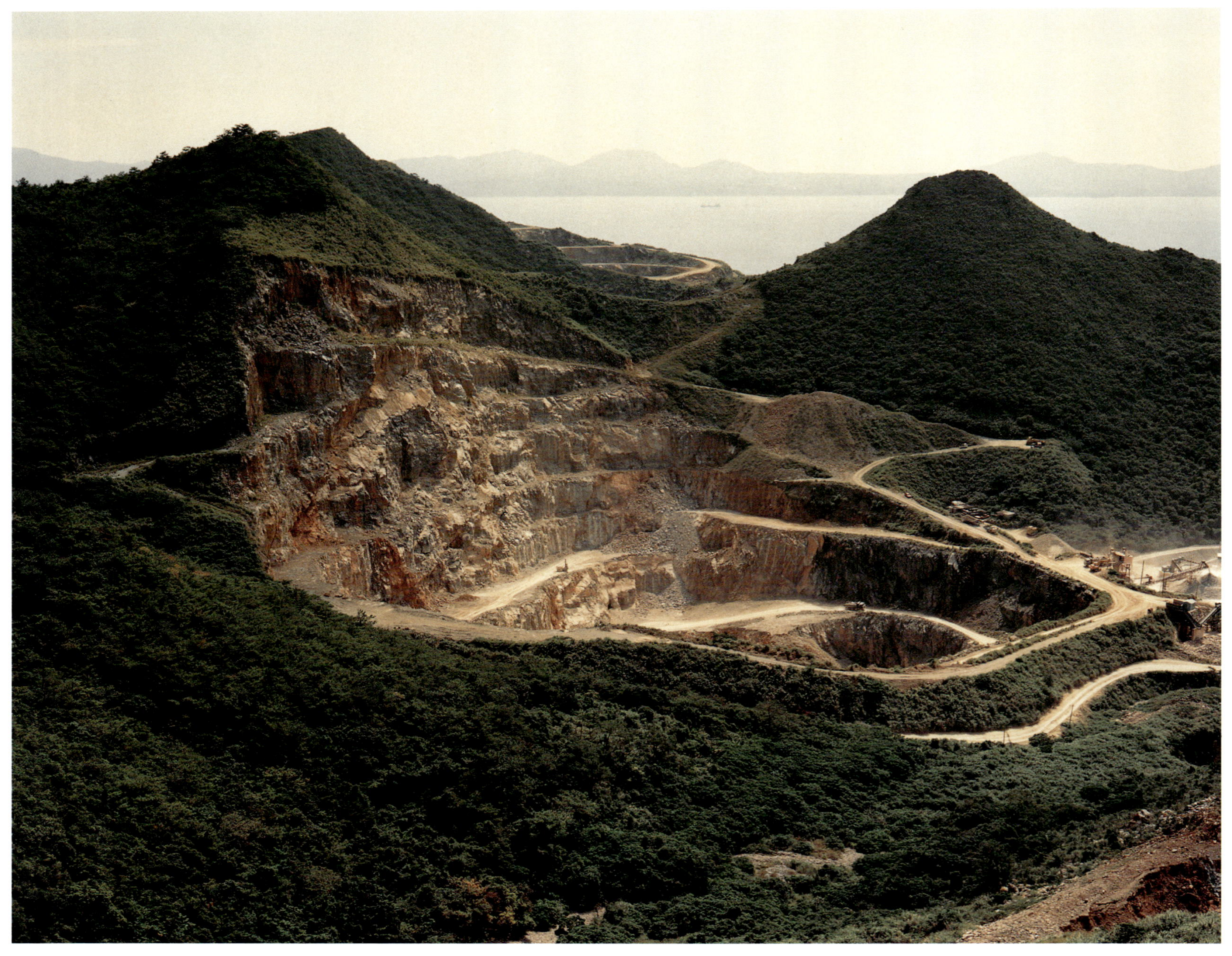

22916

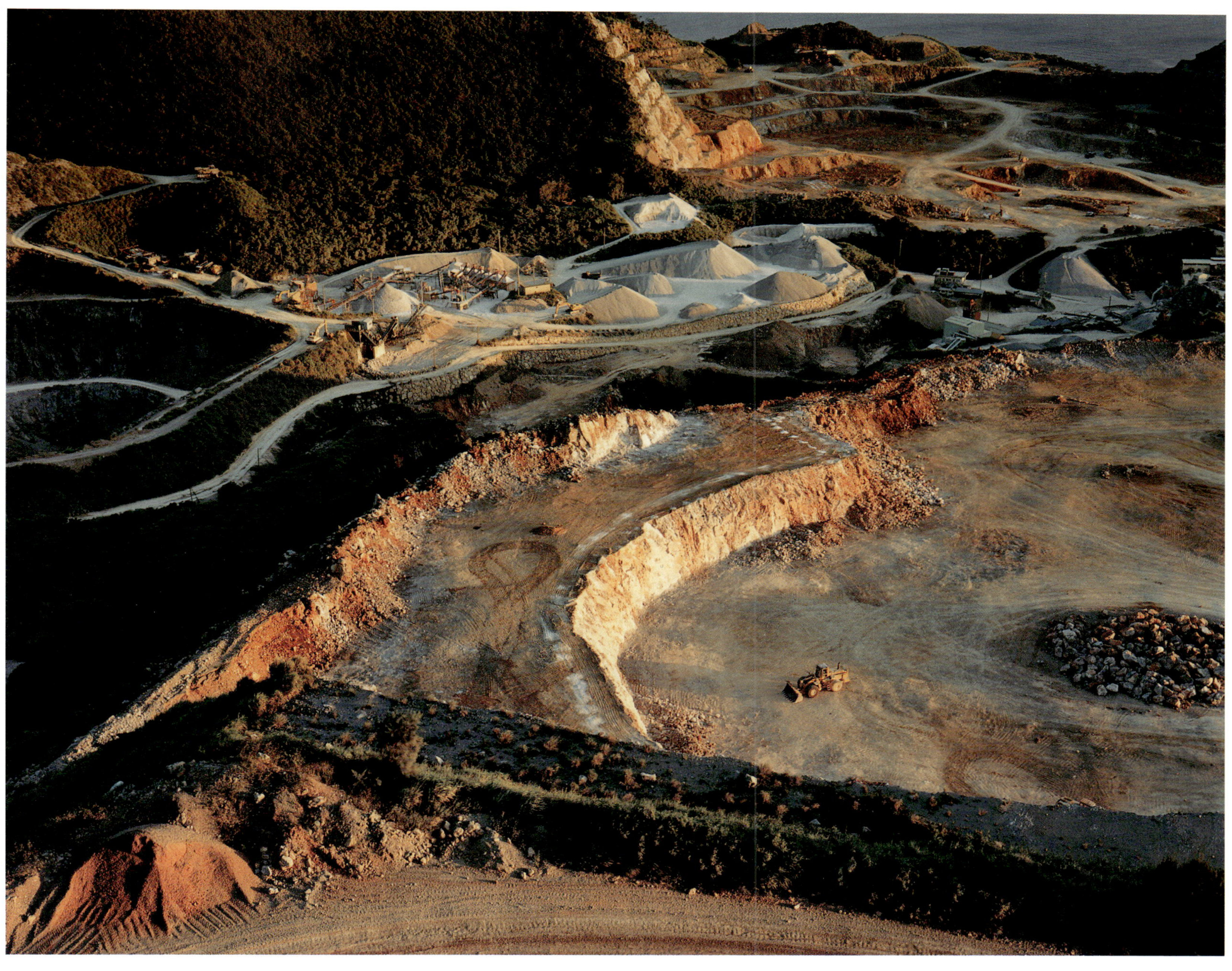

23701

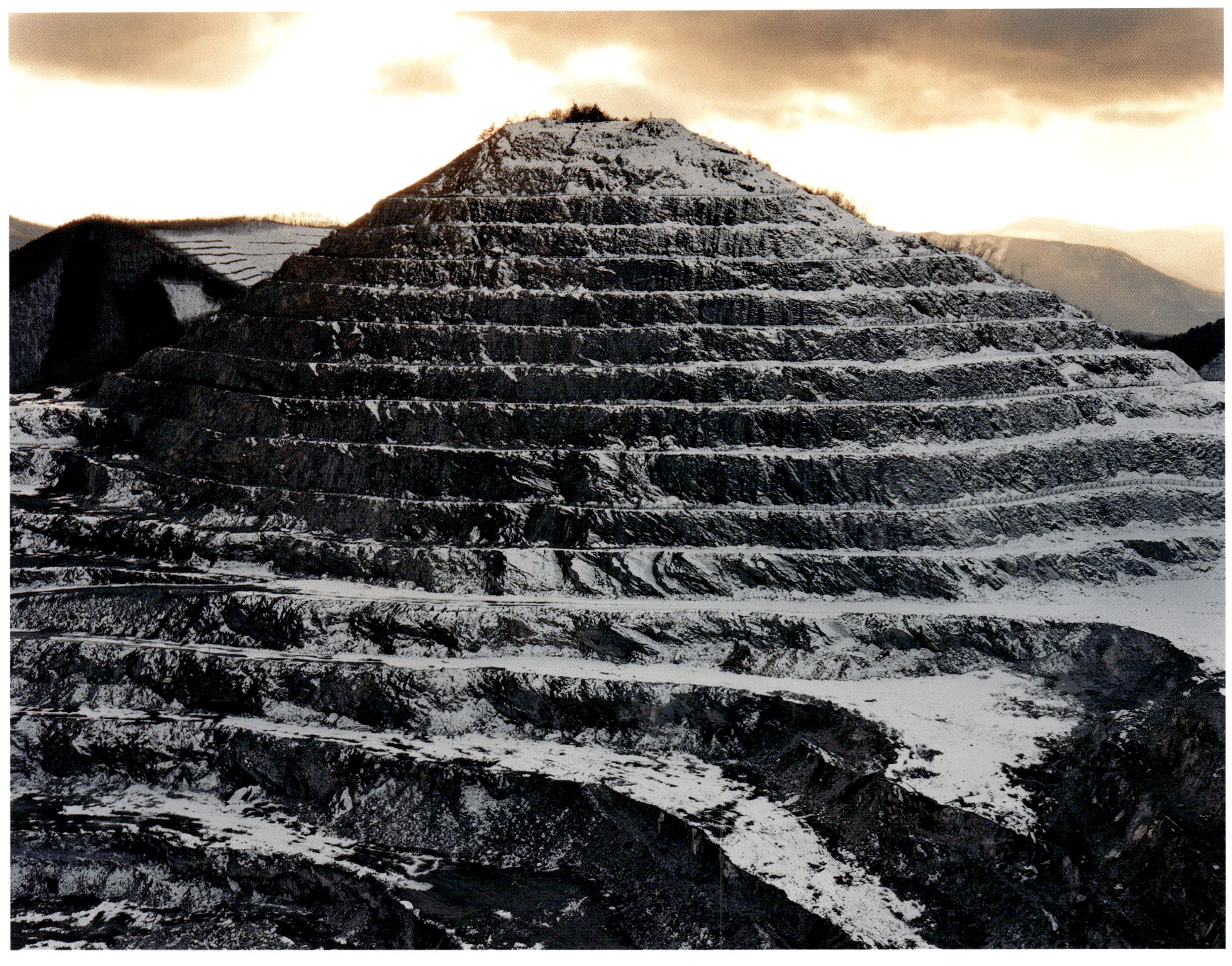

29214

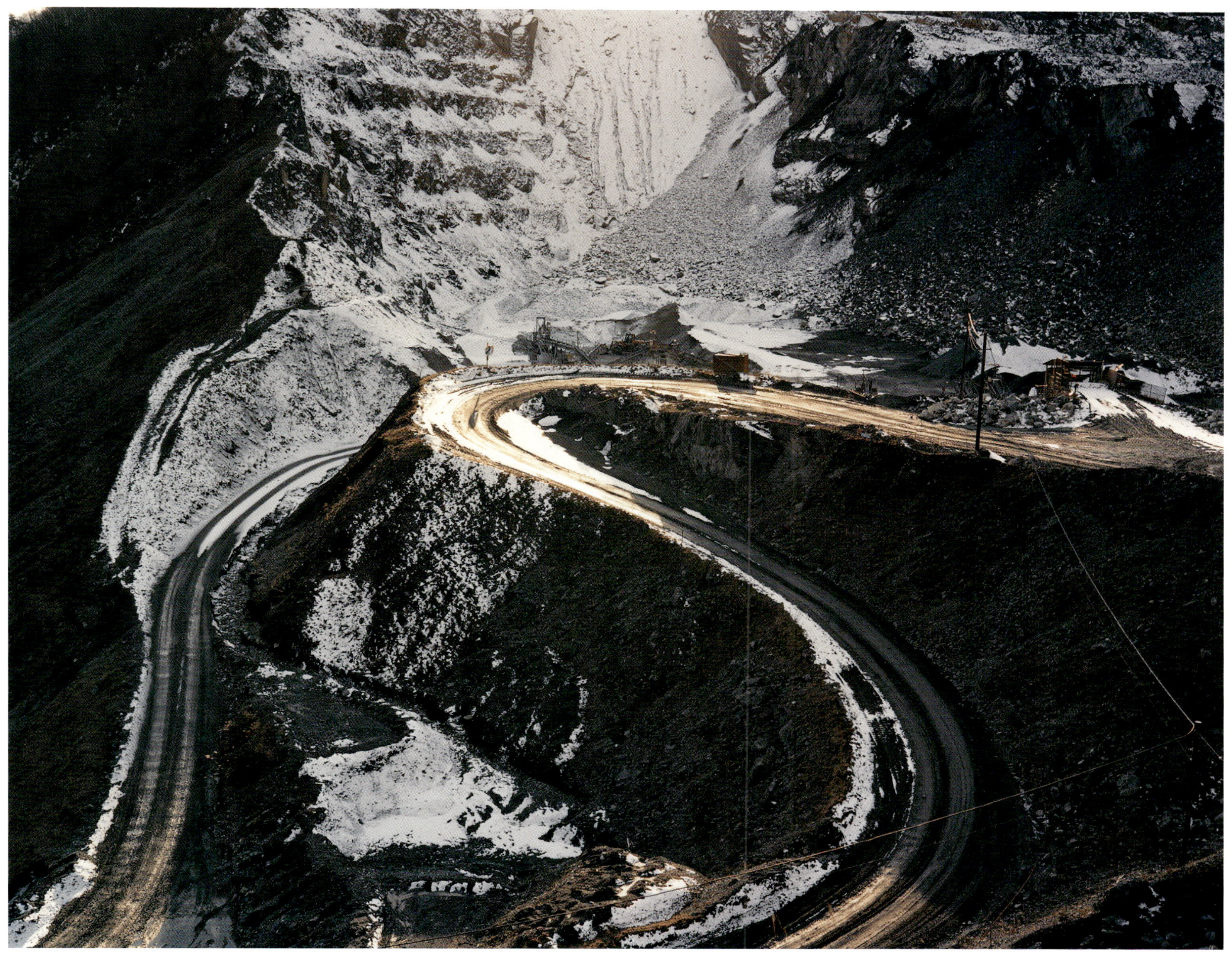

29211

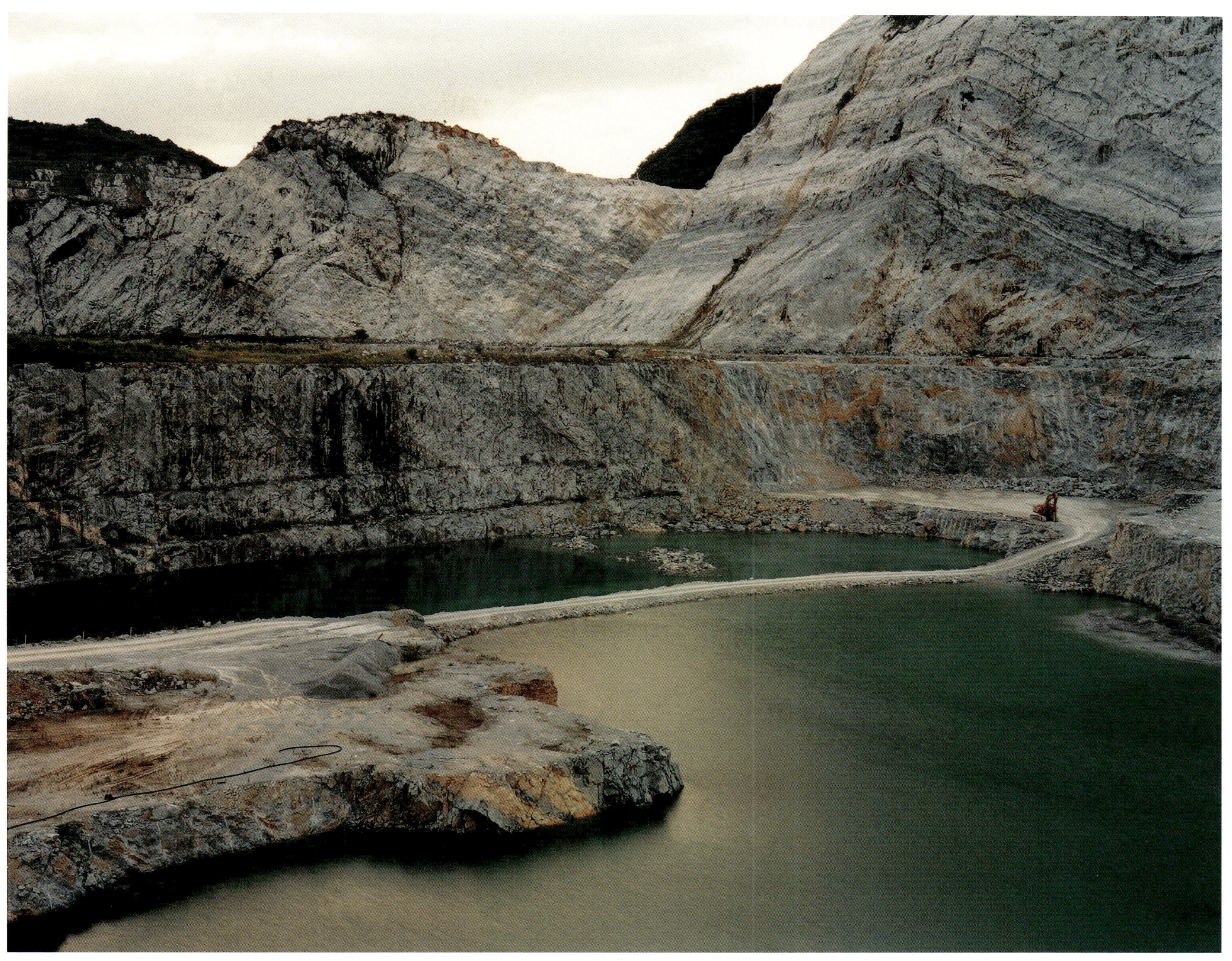

21916

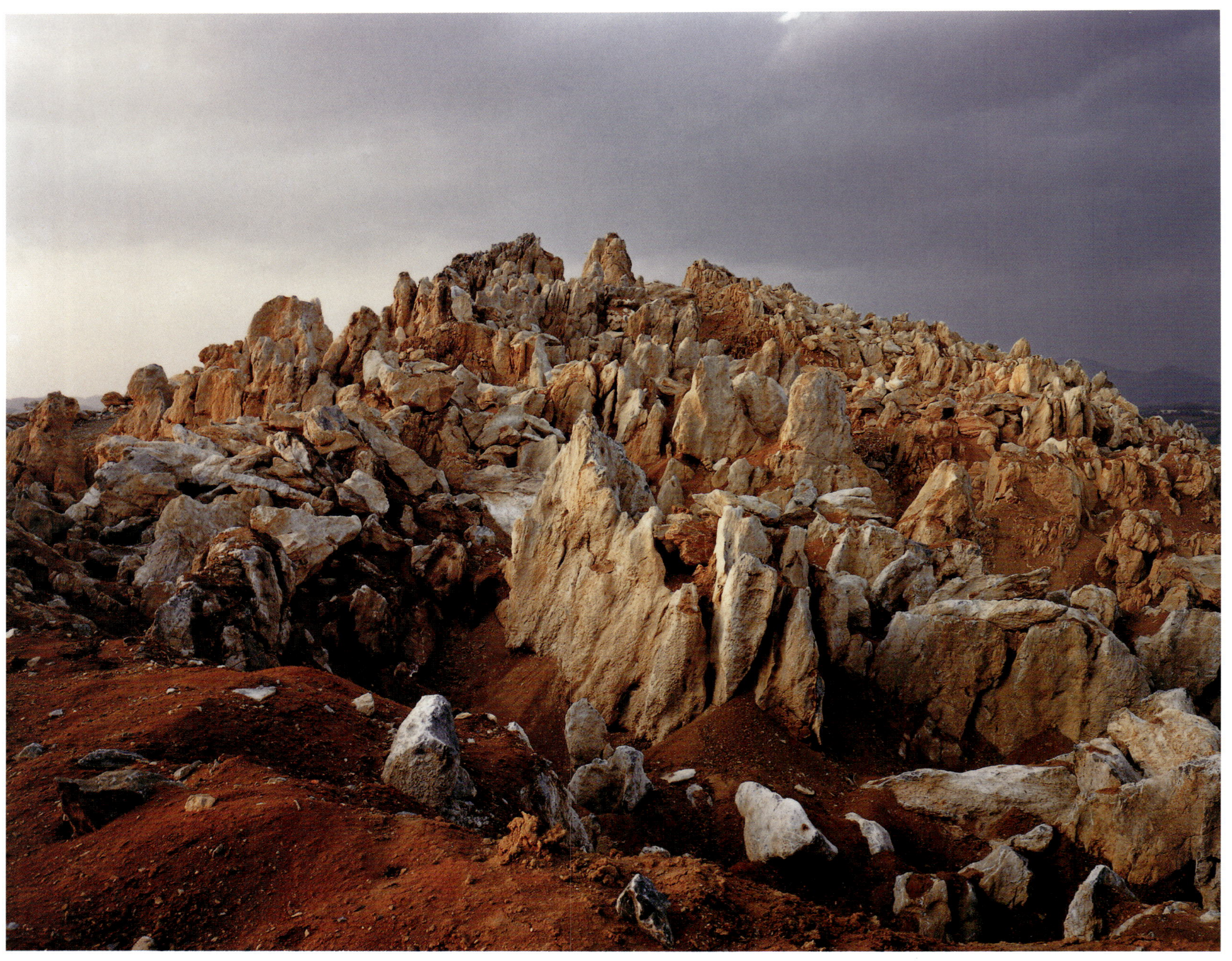

12801

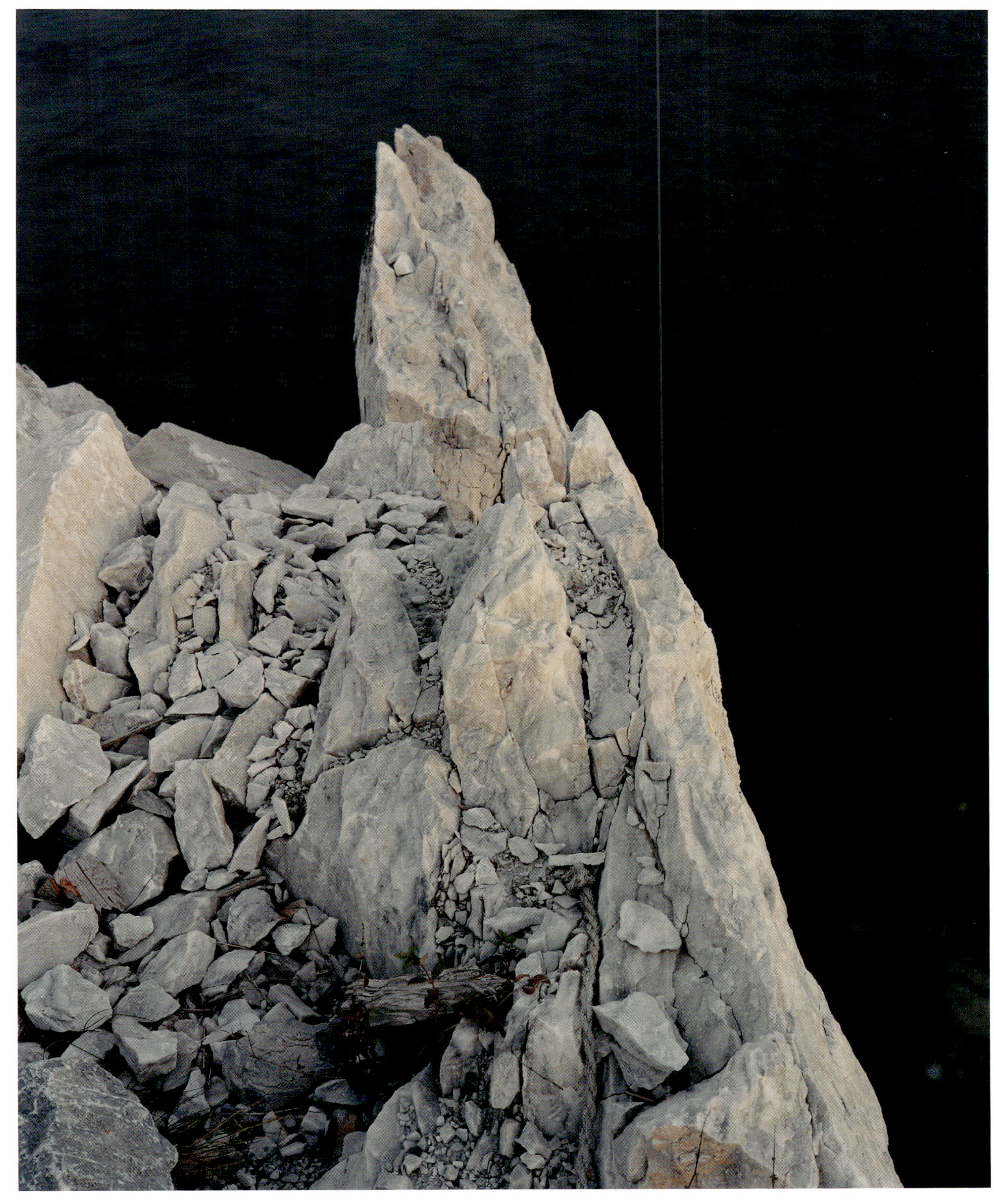

15318

Blast

Blast, since 1995, C-Print, mounted on aluminum, 100 x 150 cm

Blast, since 1995, C-Print, 38 x 57 cm

Courtesy L.A. Galerie, Frankfurt on Main; the artist

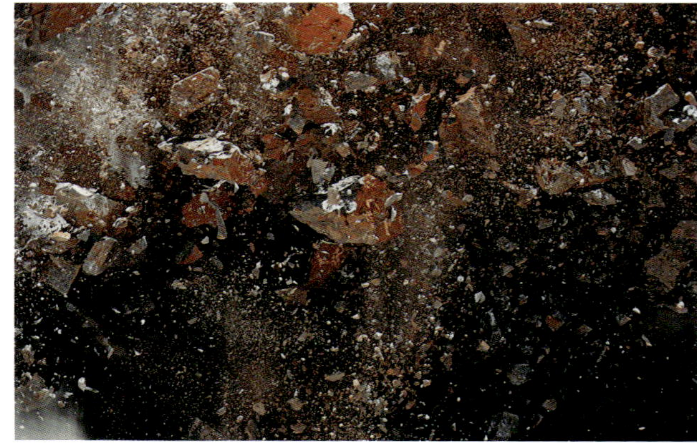

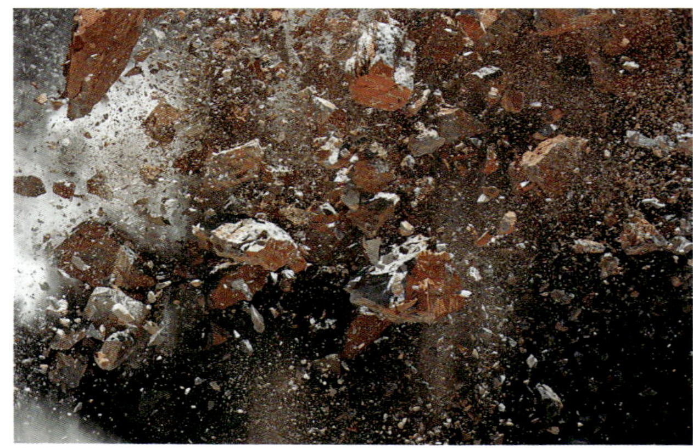

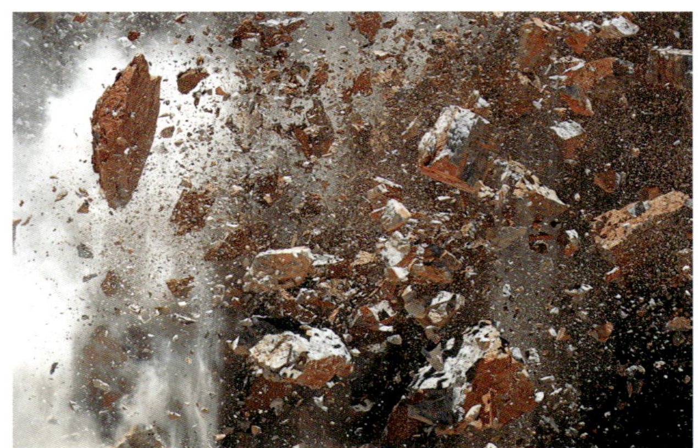

#5414 #5415 #5416

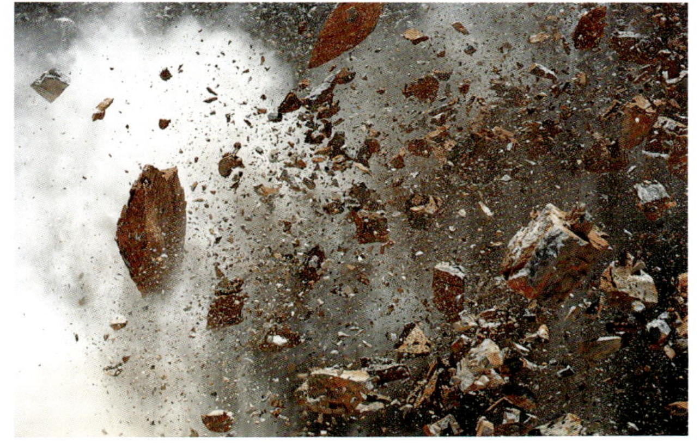

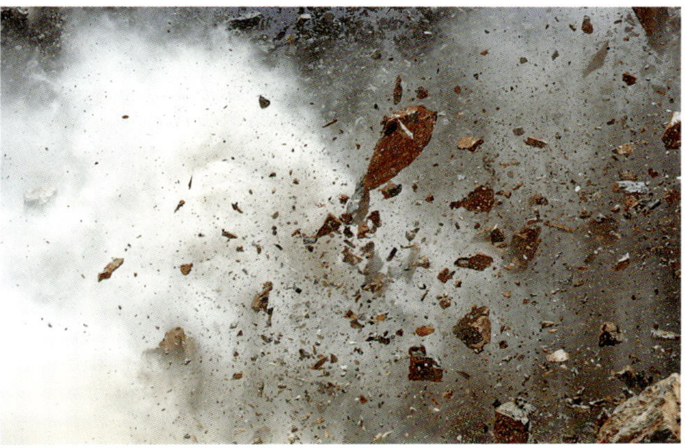

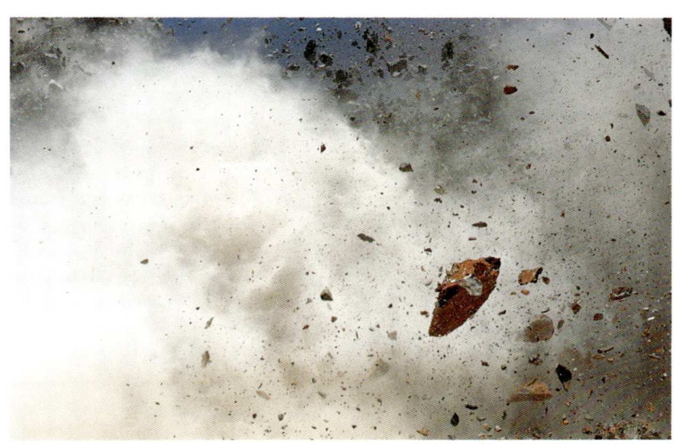

5417 # 5418 # 5419

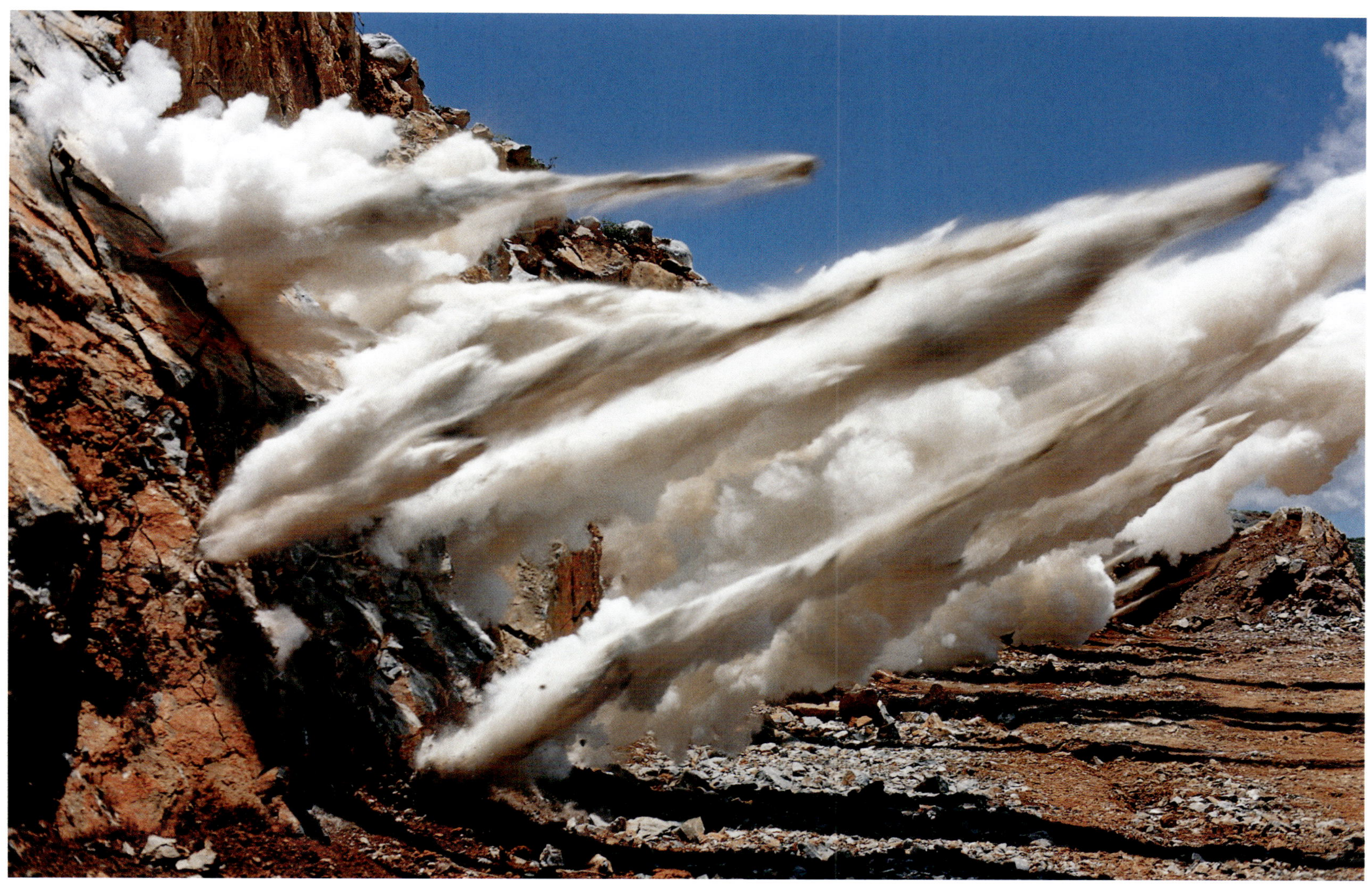

5707

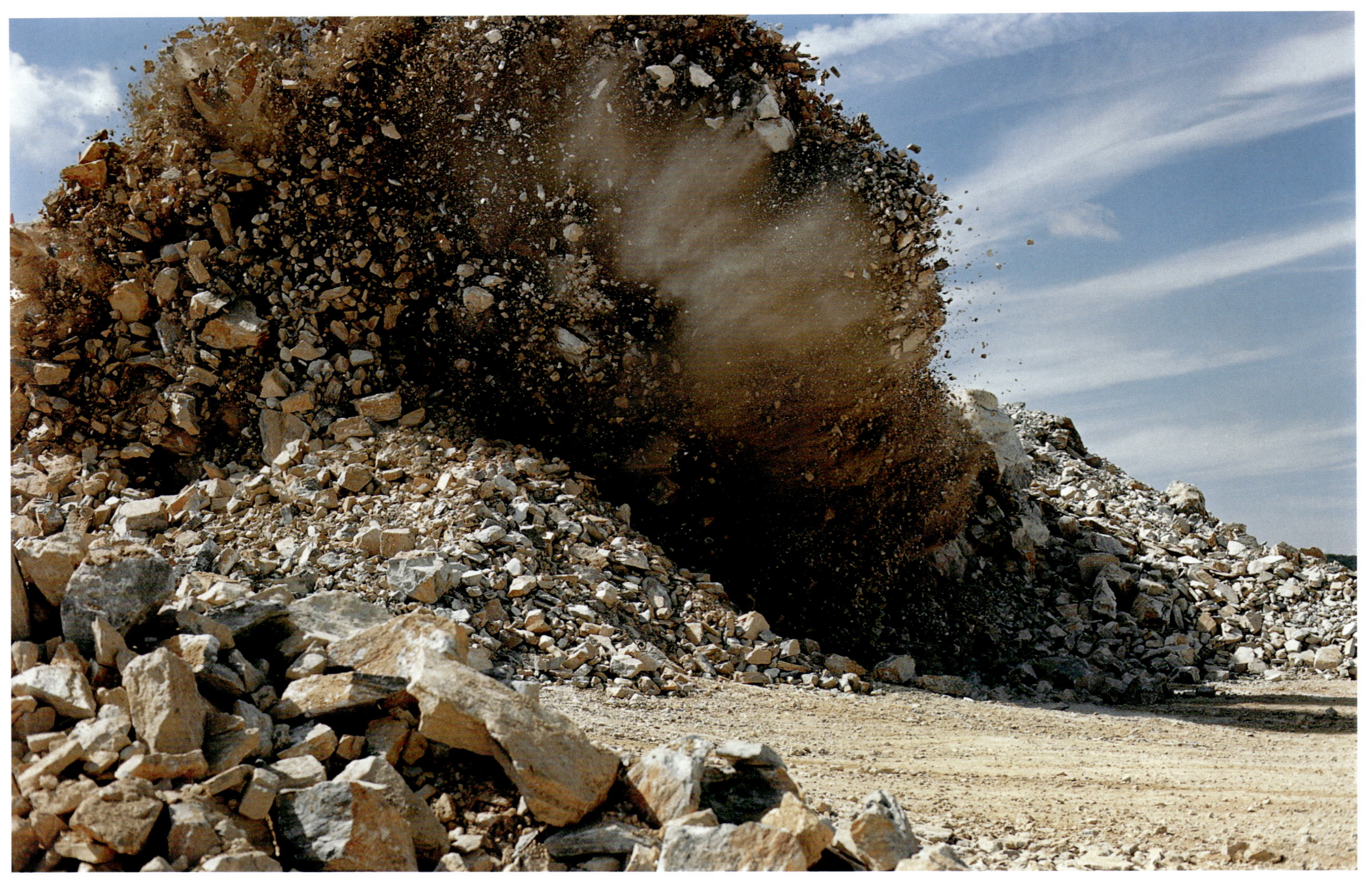

8316

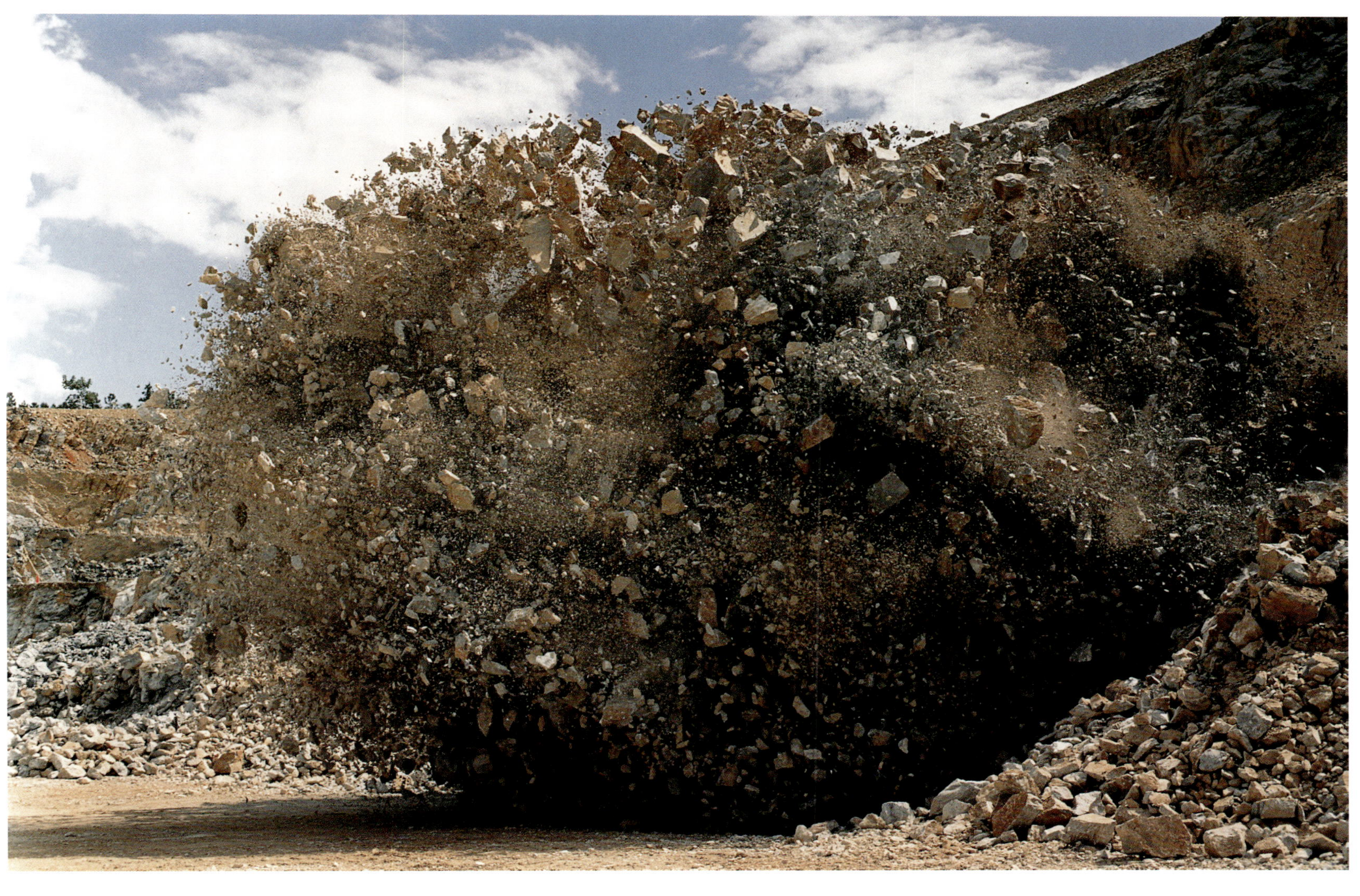

0608

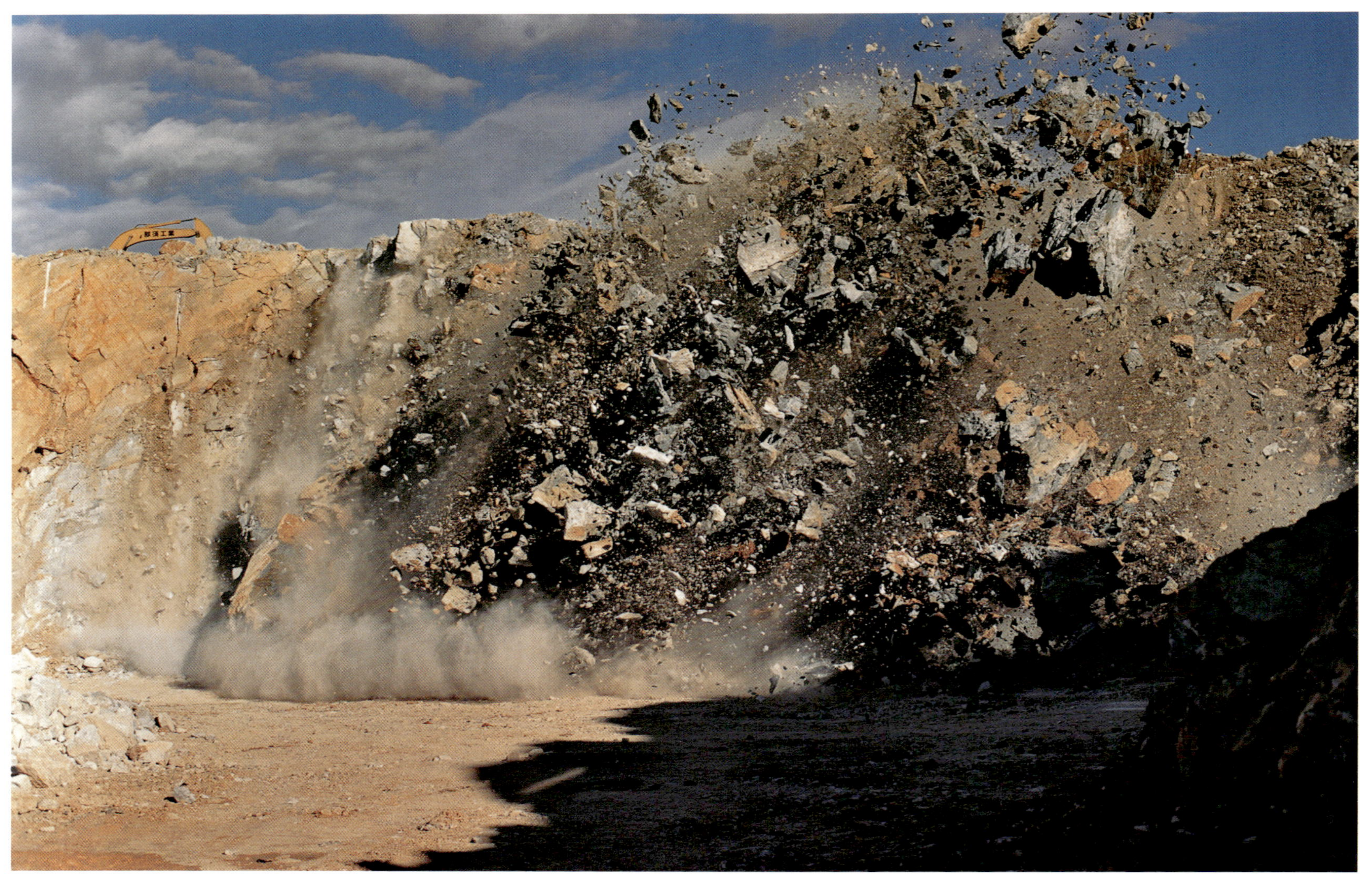

0319

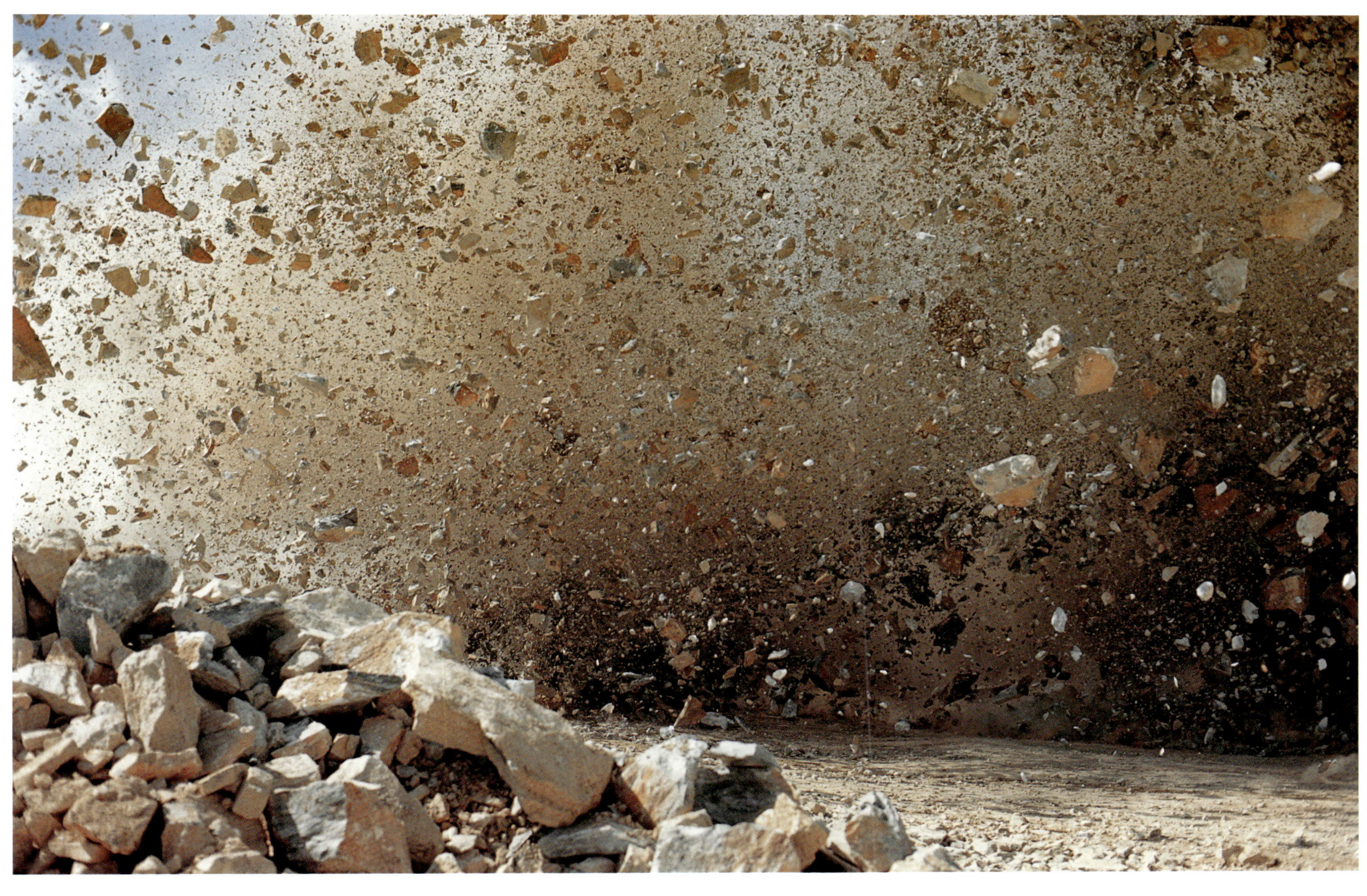

8326

River Series

A river flows below Shibuya Station. There are no fish in its shallow waters. Alone, I wade through this quiet river. Five meters above my head there are hundreds of thousands of people rushing around, talking on telephones and shopping, but there is nothing here to make me feel so. I am like an astronaut who has set foot on an uninhabited planet. (There used to be civilization on this planet. One day, however, the people who created this civilization completely vanished.) This wild daydream induces a sense of solitude and then one of freedom as I stand in the river. Later, I find solitude and freedom of the same quality in the horizontal lines of my own photographs. Although perspective, now in a state of virtual ruin, has thus far dominated the world of photography, it is this horizontal line that escapes its spells and breaks free.

I think fondly of this line and try to place myself upon it. However, a line has no space. Just as I am on the line, I realize that it occupies no space and, as if I were being swallowed up by it, I vanish too. Just like the people of the former civilization.

River Series

Unterhalb des Shibuya-Bahnhofs fließt ein Fluss. In seinem seichten Wasser leben keine Fische. Ich wate allein durch den stillen Fluss. Fünf Meter über mir sind Hunderttausende von Leuten, die hierhin und dorthin laufen, telefonieren oder einkaufen, aber hier unten ist nichts, was mich daran erinnert. Ich bewege mich wie ein Astronaut, der auf einem unbewohnten Planeten gelandet ist. Früher muss es auf diesem Planeten eine Zivilisation gegeben haben, aber die Bewohner, die diese Zivilisation errichtet hatten, sind eines Tages spurlos verschwunden. Dieser fantastische Tagtraum erfüllt mich mit einem Gefühl der Einsamkeit und auch der Freiheit, während ich in dem Fluss stehe. Später finde ich dieselbe Art von Einsamkeit und Freiheit in den horizontalen Linien meiner Fotografien. Früher war die Welt der Fotografie von der Perspektive beherrscht, doch heute ist die Perspektive fast völlig zerfallen, und die Horizontale ist aus ihrem Bann in die Freiheit entkommen.

Ich denke gerne an diese Linie und versuche, mich auf ihr zu situieren. Aber eine Linie hat keinen Raum. Sowie ich auf der Linie bin, erkenne ich, dass sie keinen Raum einnimmt, und als würde ich von ihr verschlungen, verschwinde ich ebenfalls. So wie die Menschen der vergangenen Zivilisation.

River Series, 1993–94,
C-Print, mounted on aluminum, 100 x 49 cm
Private Collection

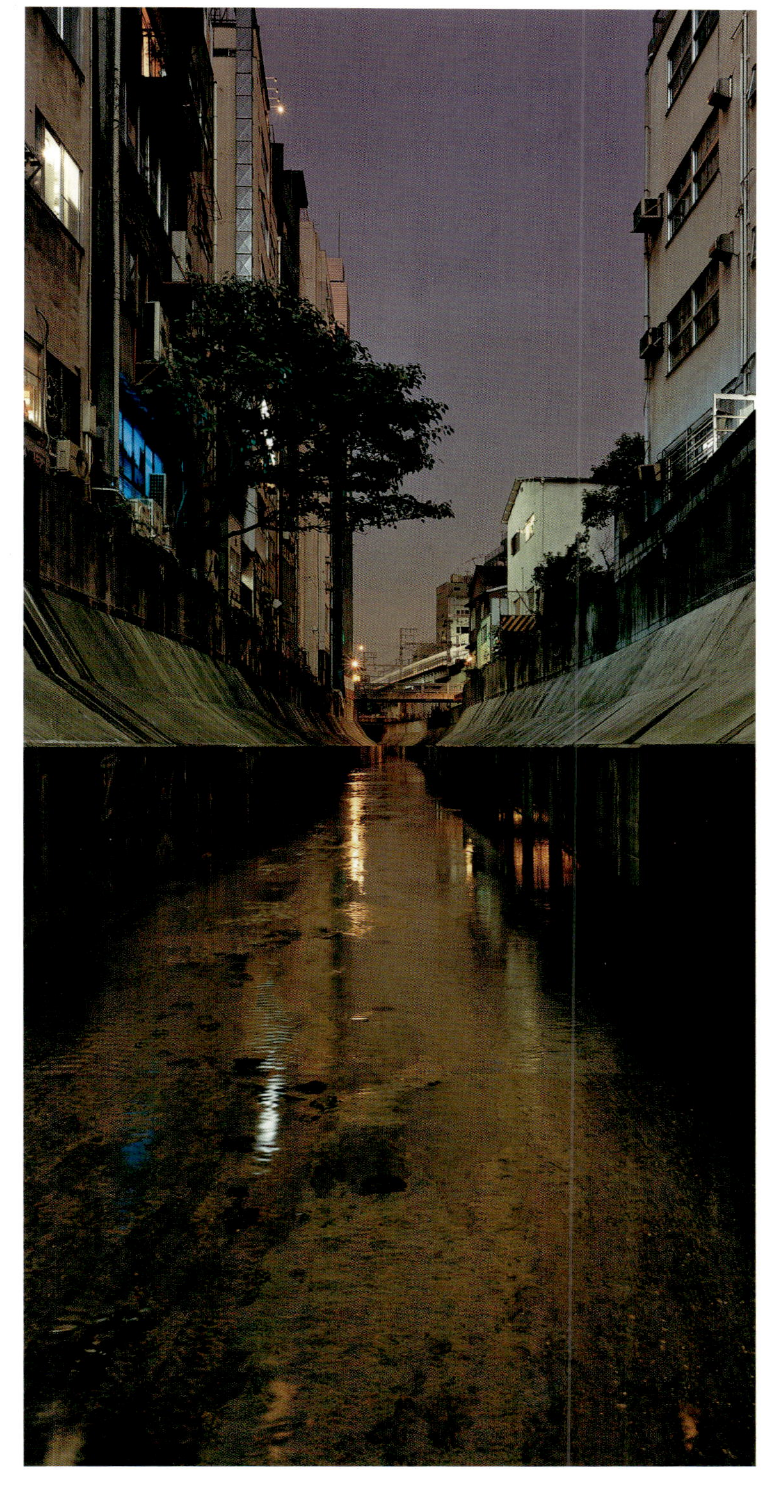

1

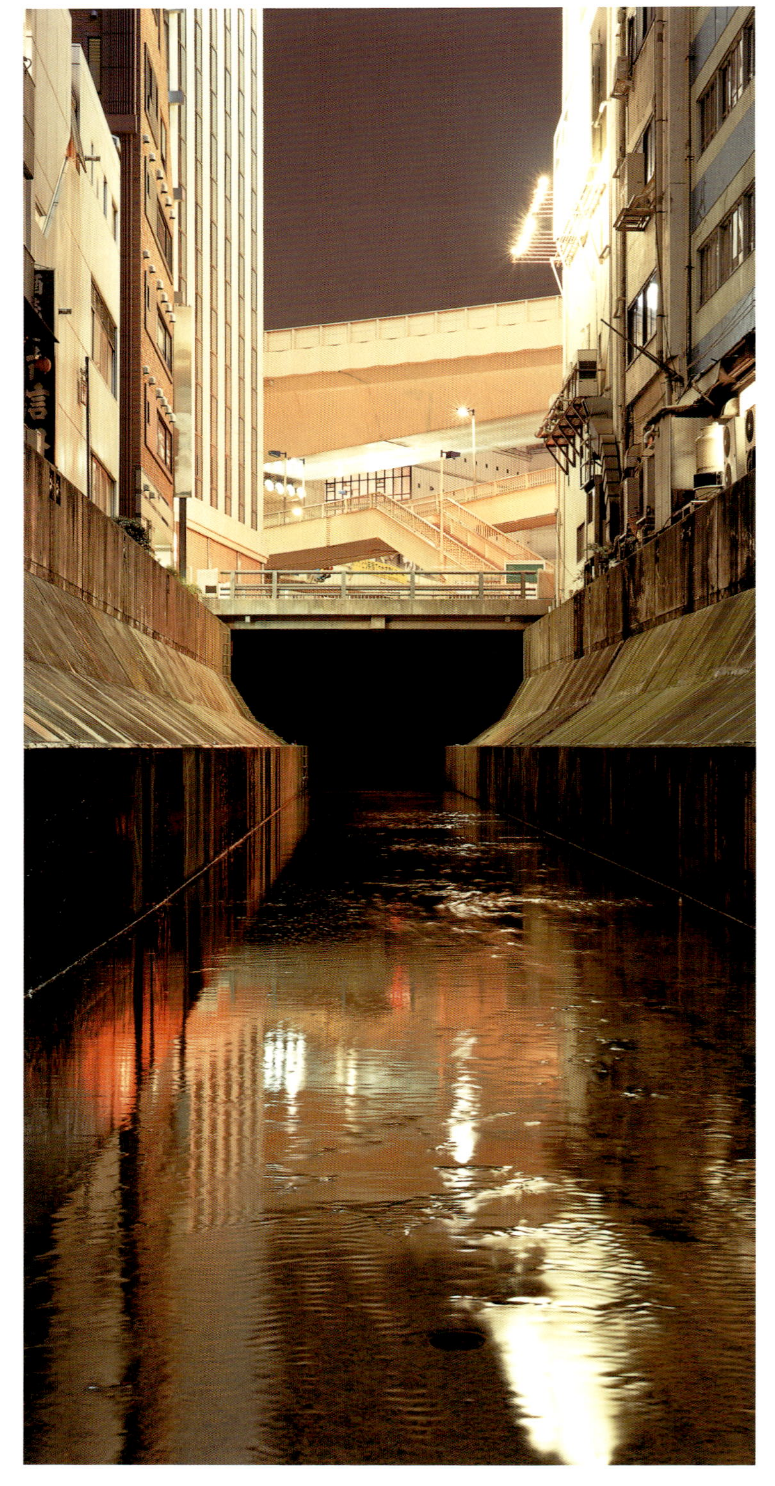

#2

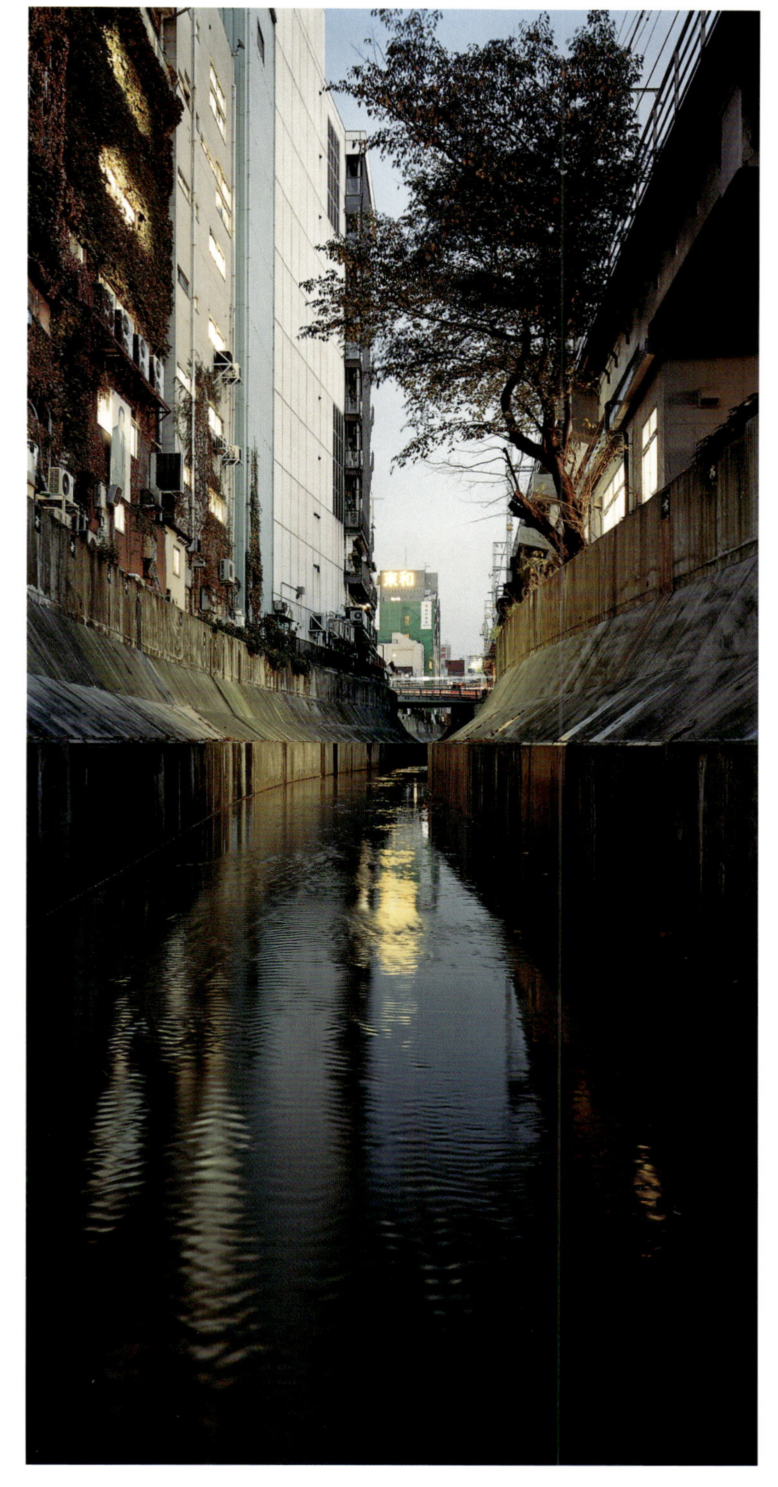

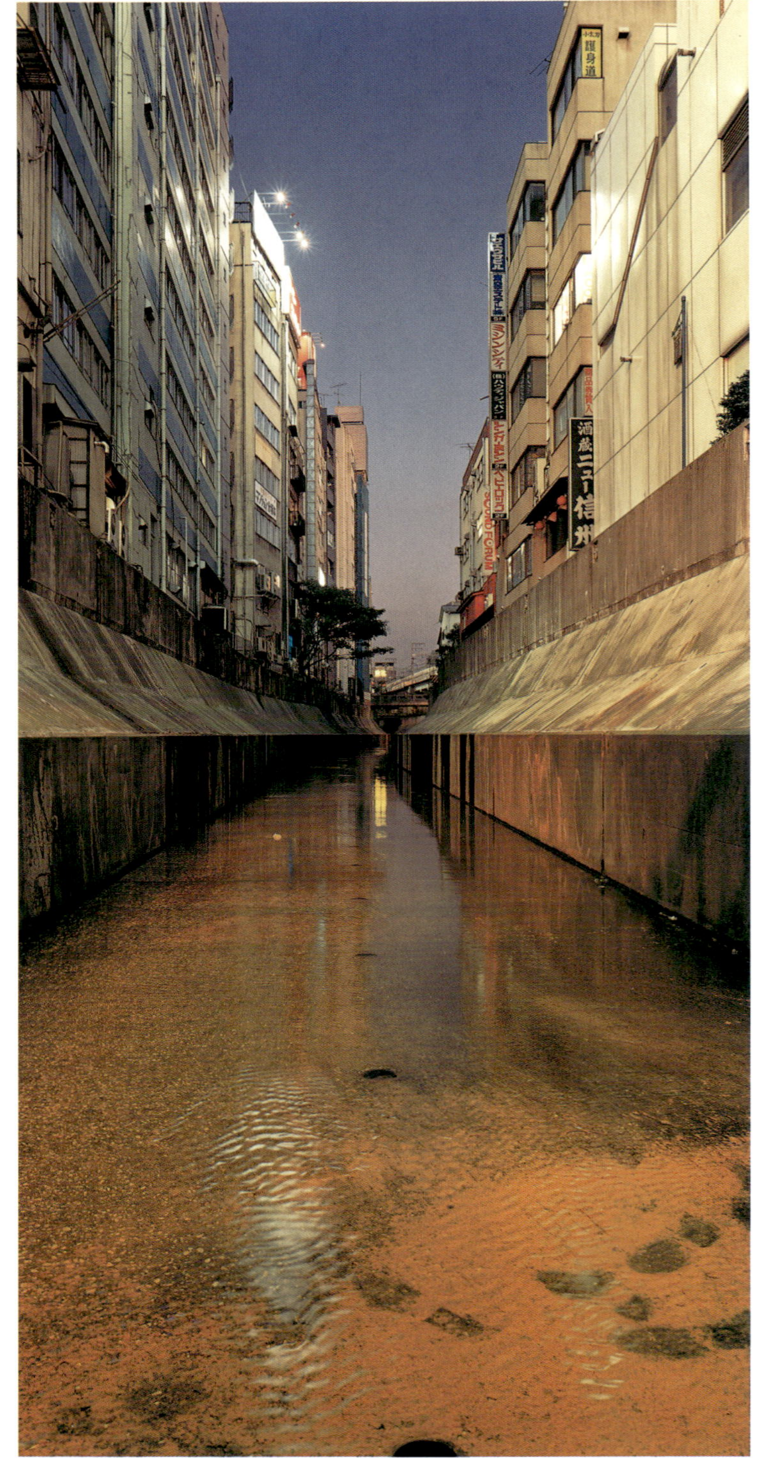

#4

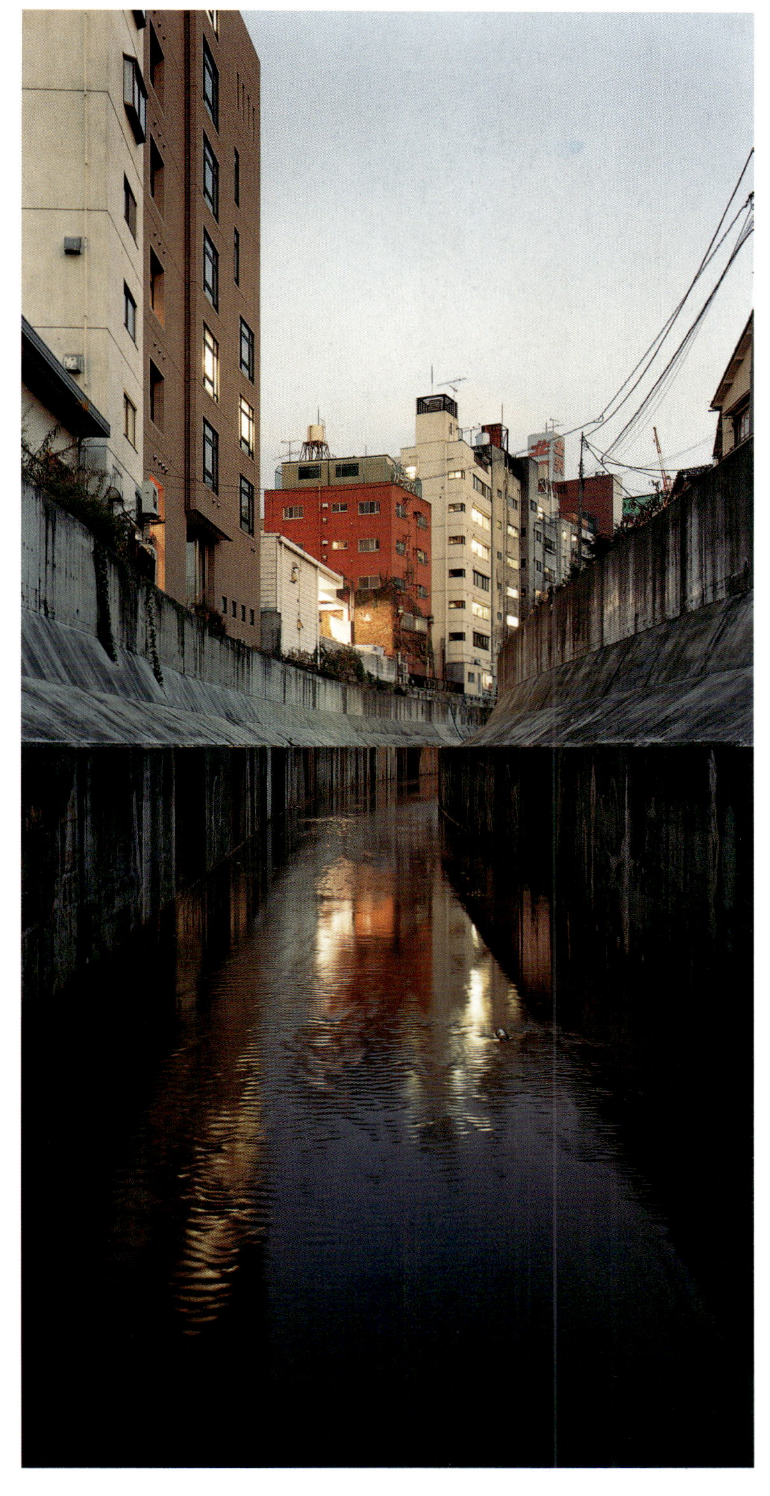

#5

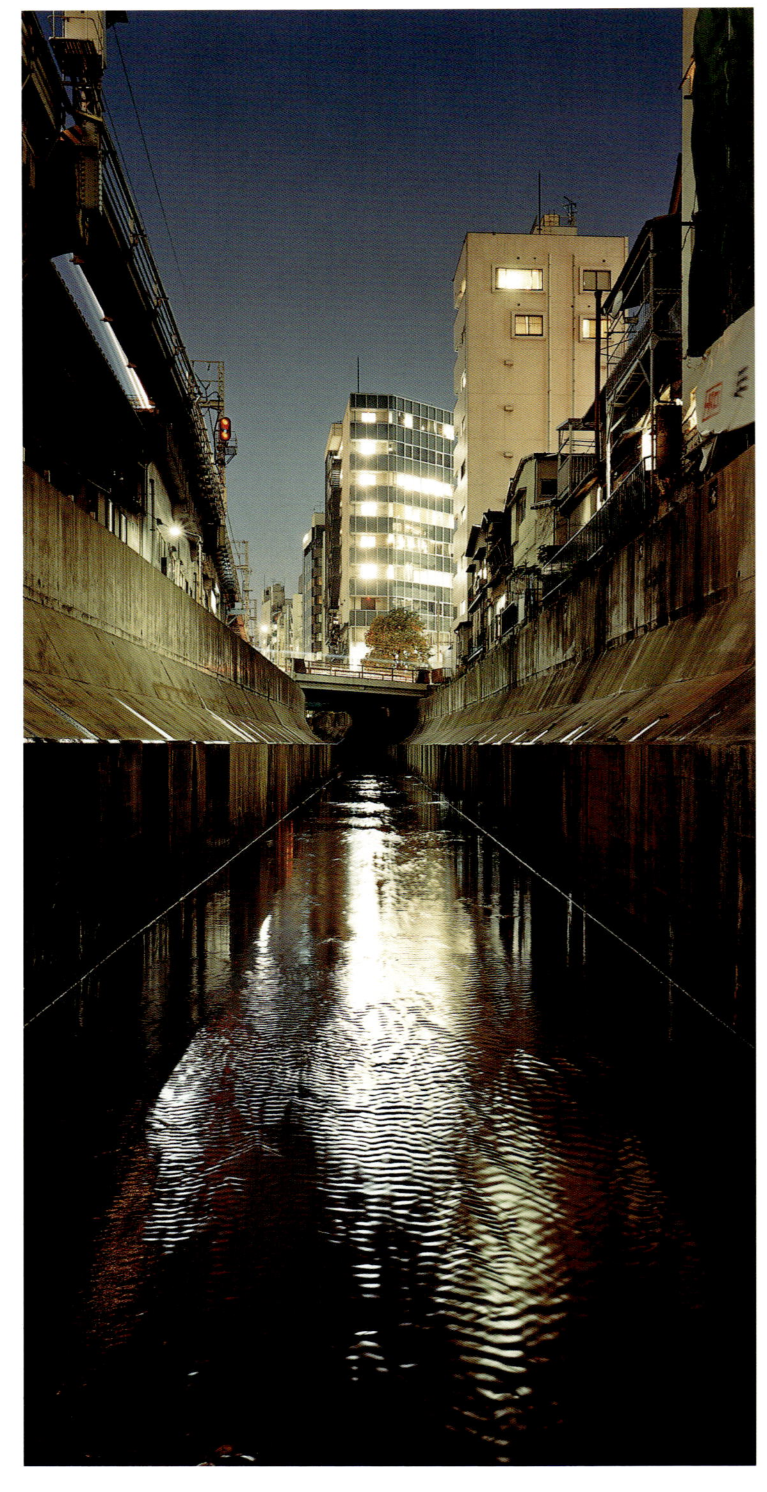

#6

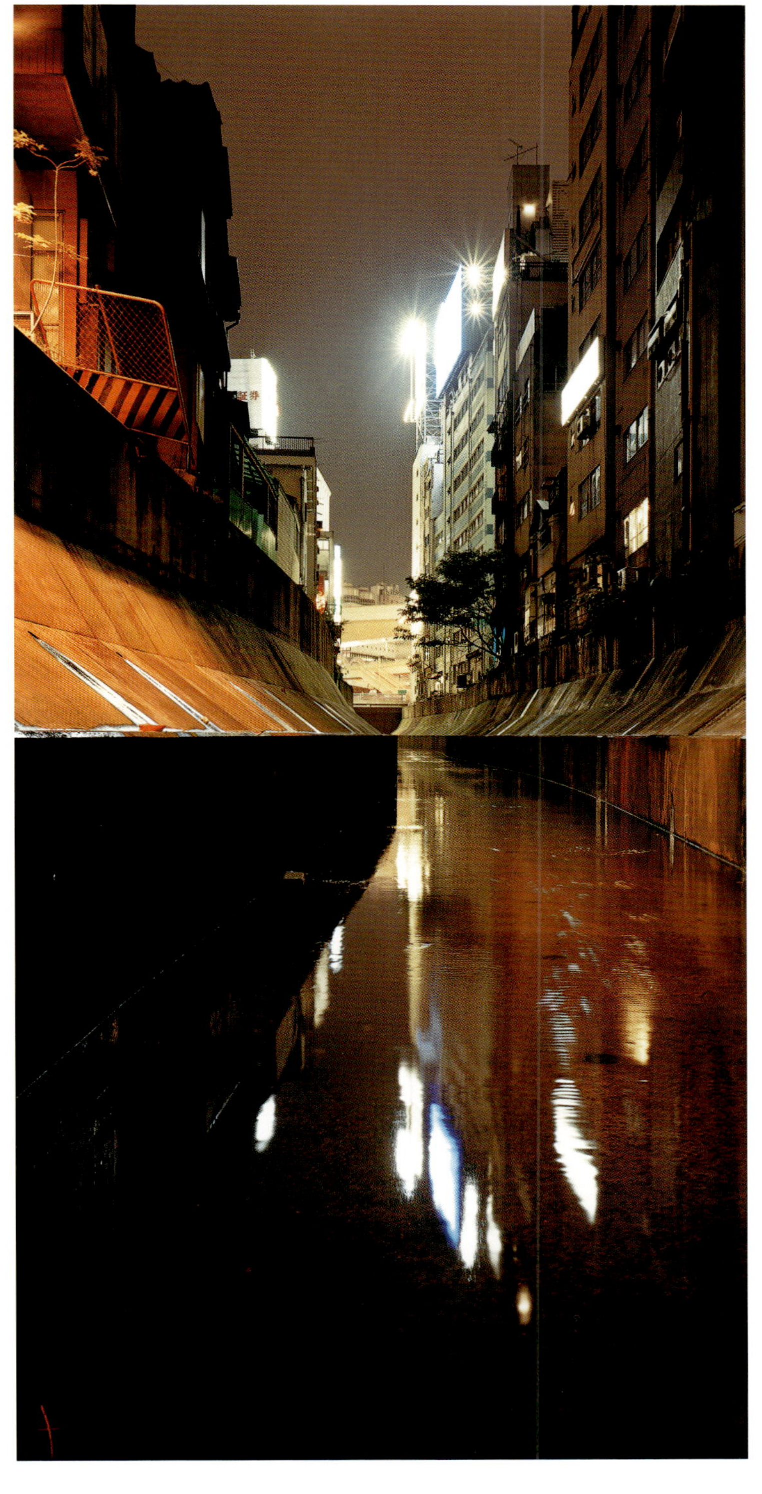

7

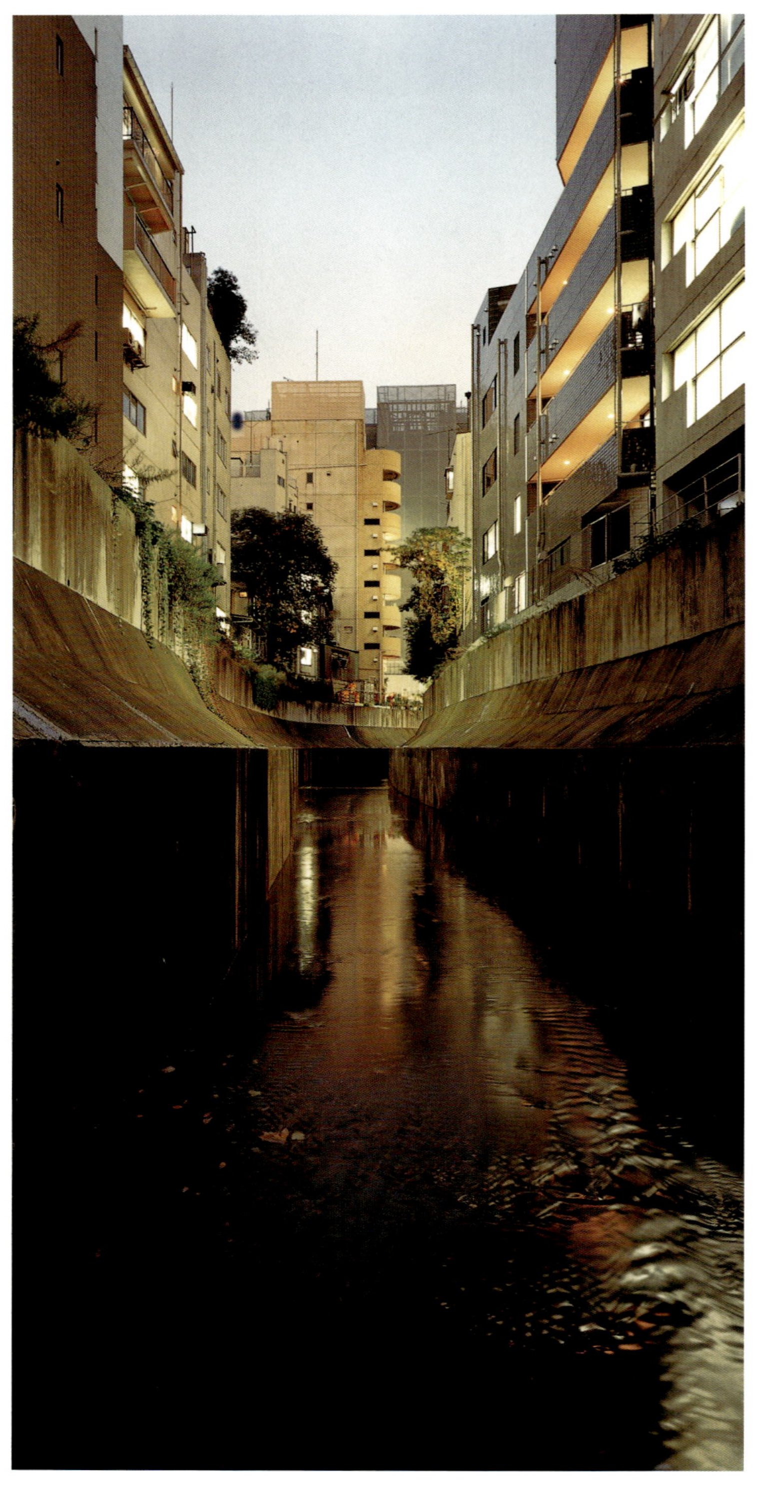

8

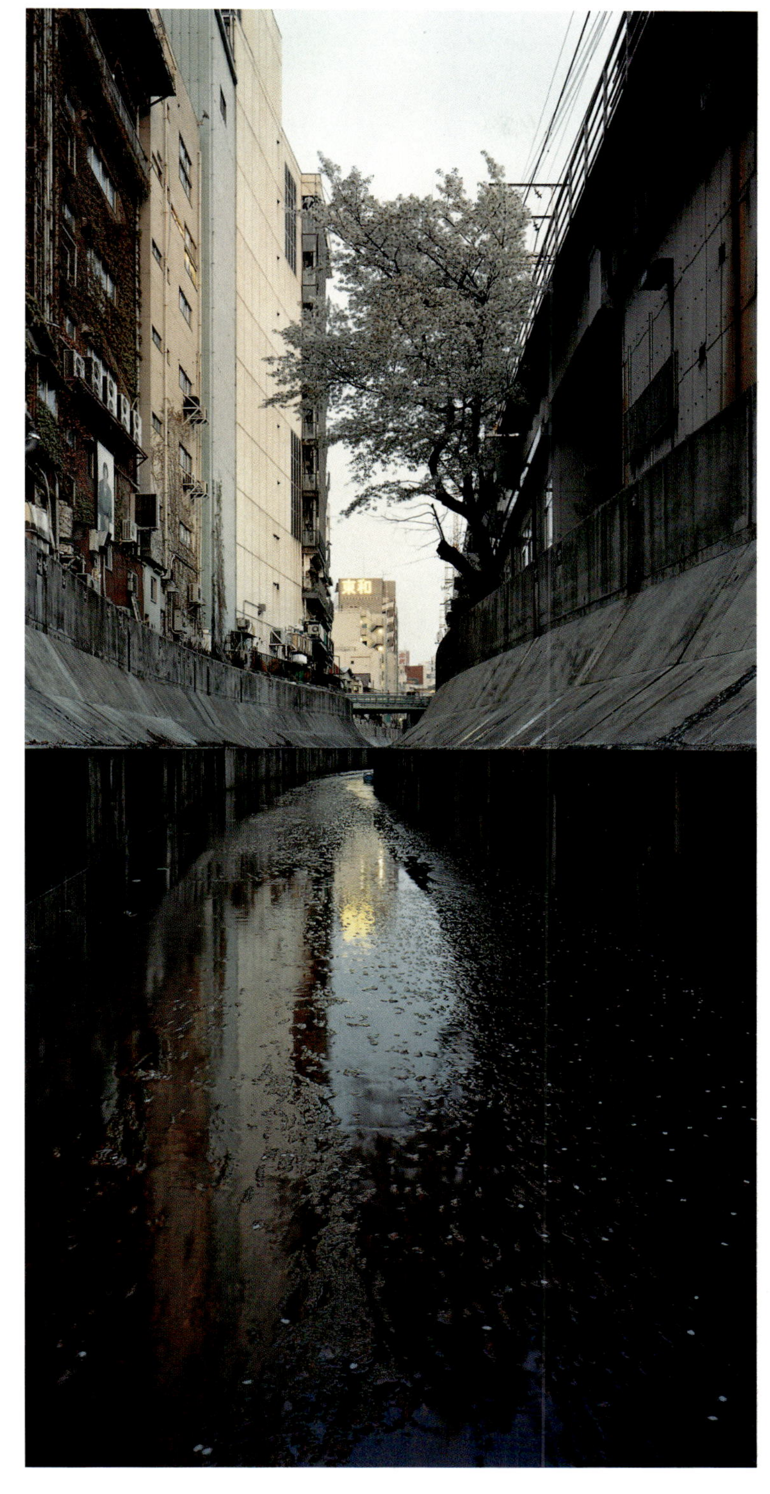

Underground

Underground it is always pitch black.
Even if the light that I bring with me brings out some kind of form or coloration, to those things that exist in the underground world, it is inconsequential.
When the light fades, the form and coloration of these things dissolve like a phantom. The things of the underground exist inside a perfect darkness, oblivious to the light and sense of vision of the world above ground.
They are completely uninterested in the process of "watching being watched." Incidentally, isn't it true that "nature" is also one of these things that is absolutely uninterested in "humans"?
If so, the water that flows in the pitch black underground and the small organisms that live there are twice as uninterested in "humans" and are all the more "nature."
This place is unimaginably far away from "humans" even if hundreds of thousands of people are living their life right above it.

Underground

Im Untergrund ist es immer pechschwarz.
Auch wenn die Lampe, die ich bei mir habe, so etwas wie Formen und Farben sichtbar macht, ist sie für die Dinge, die in dieser unterirdischen Welt leben, ohne Bedeutung.
Wenn das Licht schwächer wird, verschwinden die Formen und Farben der Dinge wie ein Phantom. Die Dinge des Untergrunds leben in vollkommener Dunkelheit, ohne Bewusstsein des Lichts und ohne die Sehkraft der oberirdischen Welt.
Es interessiert sie nicht im Geringsten zu beobachten, wie sie beobachtet werden. Ist es nicht überhaupt so, dass die »Natur« völlig desinteressiert an den »Menschen« ist?
Aber dann ist das Wasser, das in diesem pechschwarzen Untergrund fließt, und dann sind die Kleinorganismen, die hier leben, doppelt so desinteressiert an den »Menschen«, aber dafür umso mehr »Natur«.
Dieser Ort ist unvorstellbar weit von den »Menschen« entfernt, selbst wenn Hunderttausende von ihnen direkt darüber leben.

Underground/River (Tunnel Series), 1999, C-Print, 49 x 49 cm
Courtesy L.A. Galerie, Frankfurt on Main; the artist

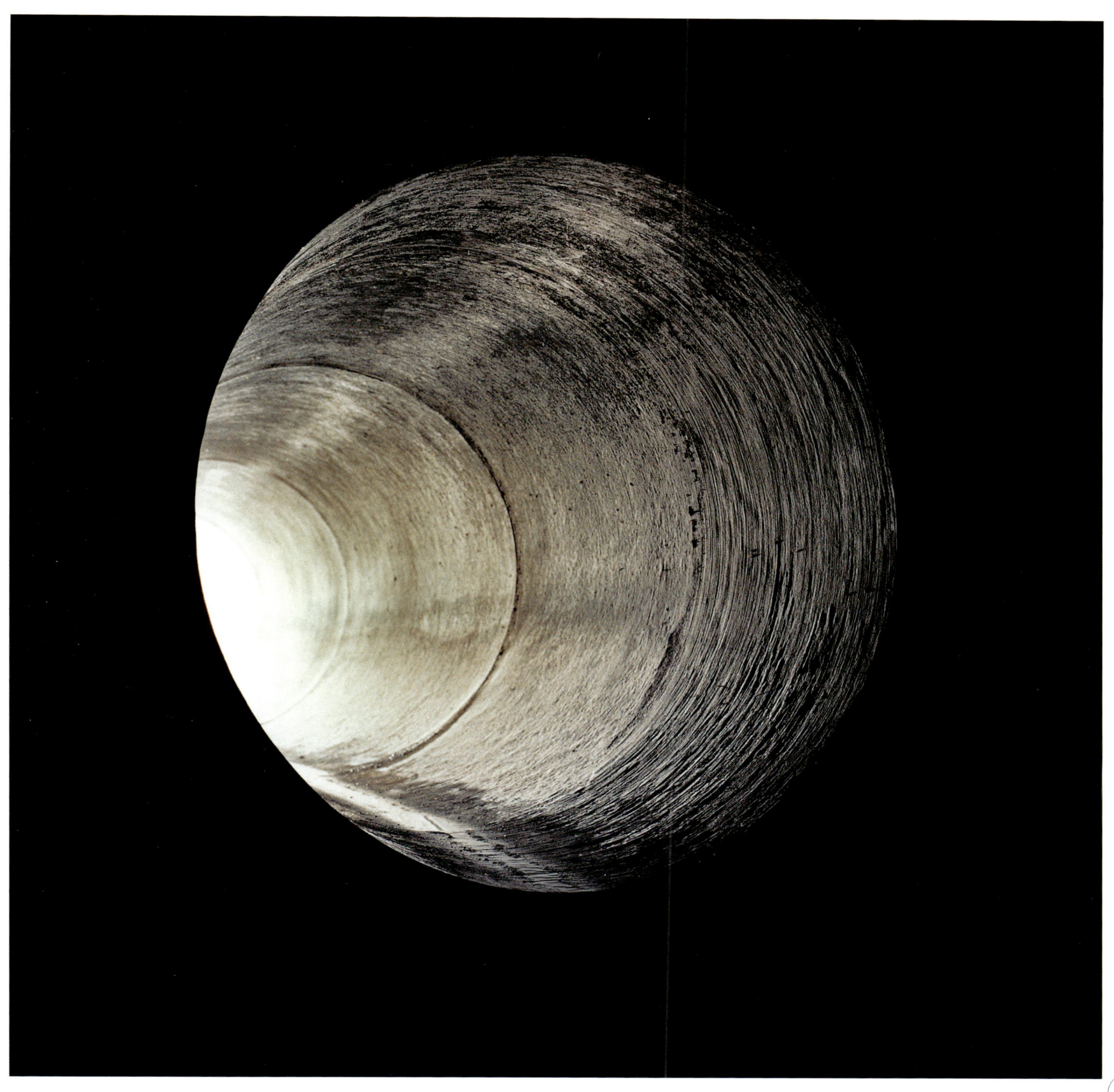

6109

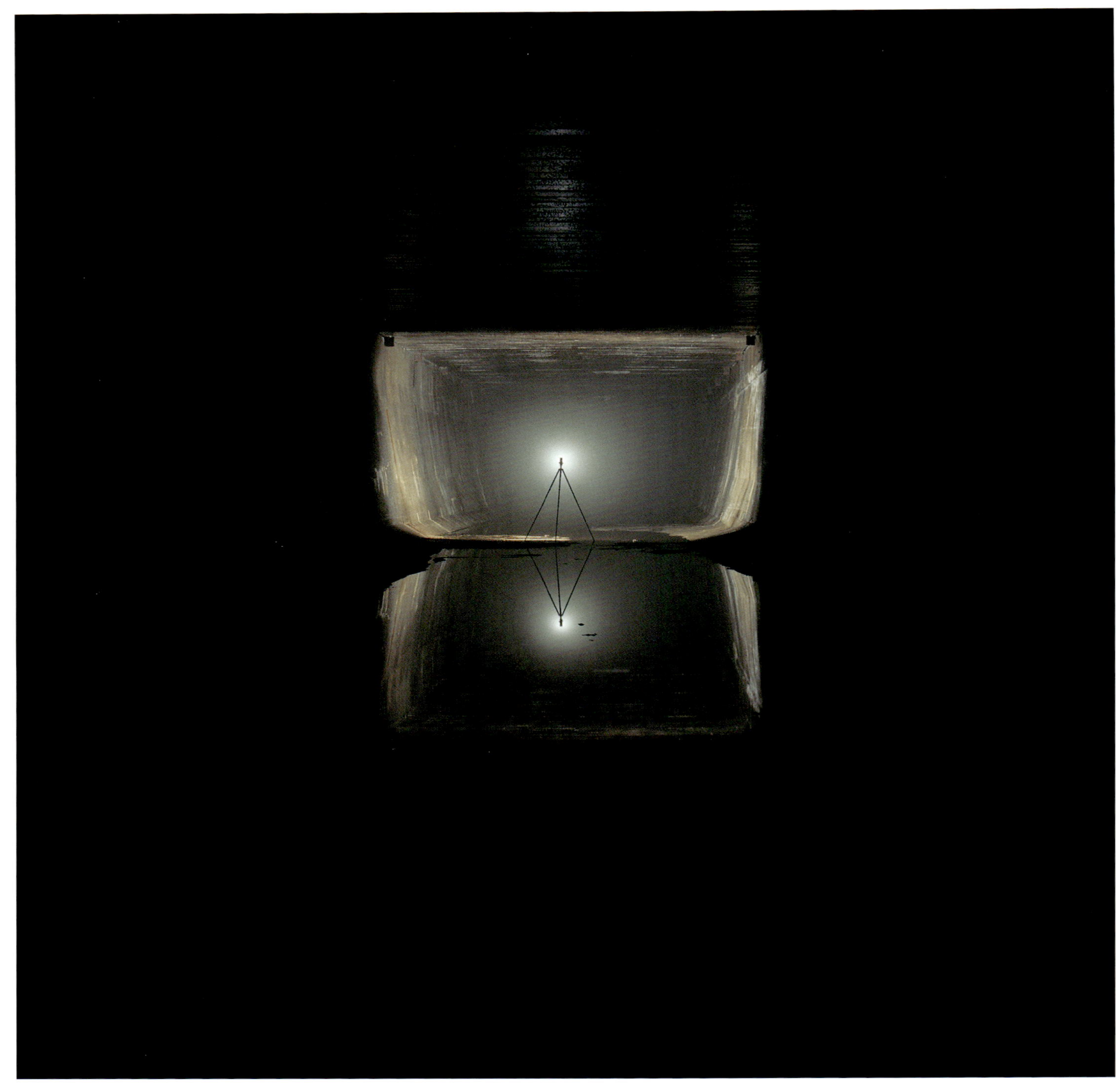

6912

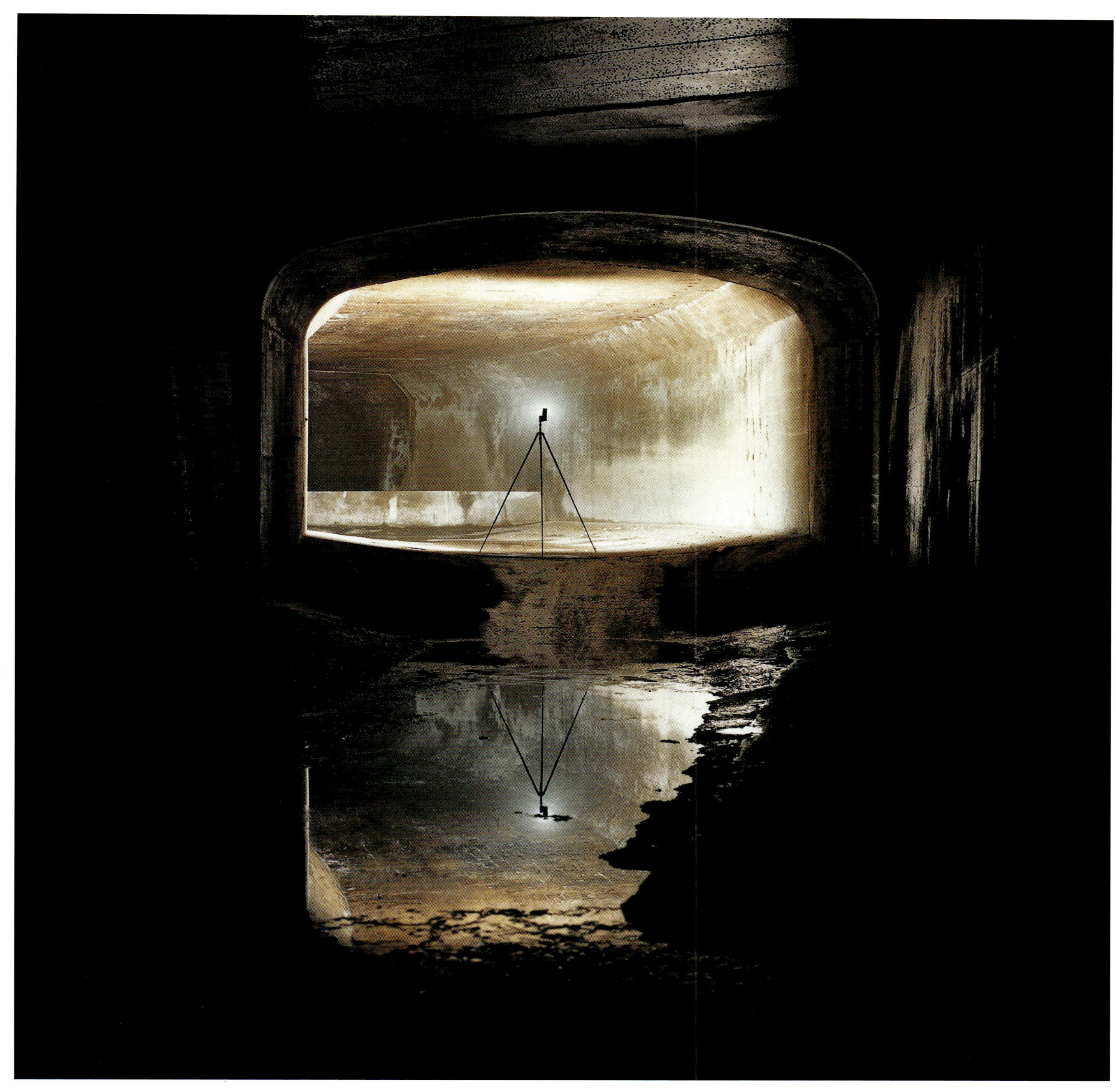

6411

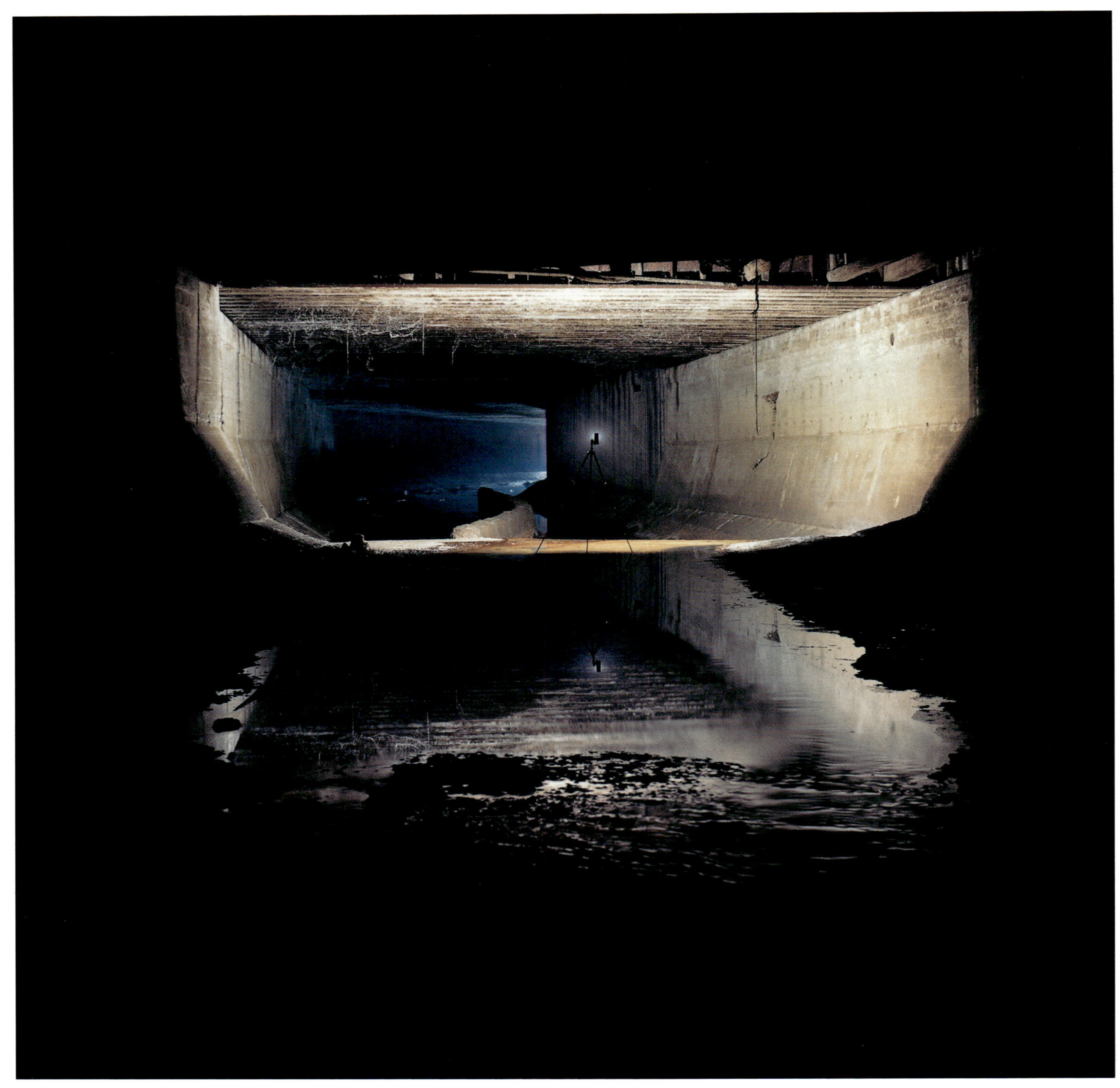

6205

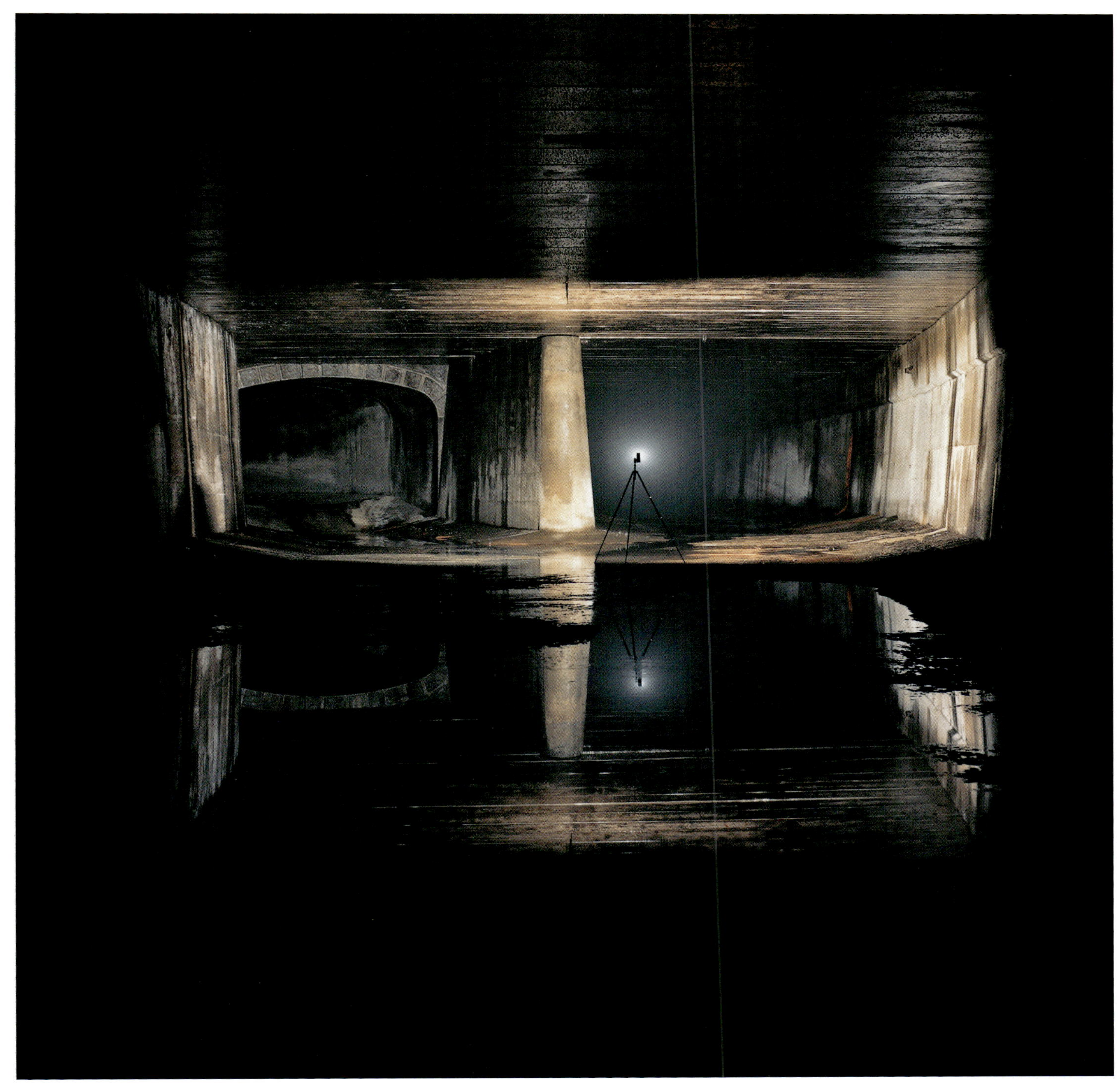

6303

Underground

Underground/Water, 1999,
C-Print, mounted on aluminum, 110 x 110 cm
Courtesy L.A. Galerie, Frankfurt on Main; the artist; Kunstsammlung der DZ BANK AG, Frankfurt on Main (# 3108)

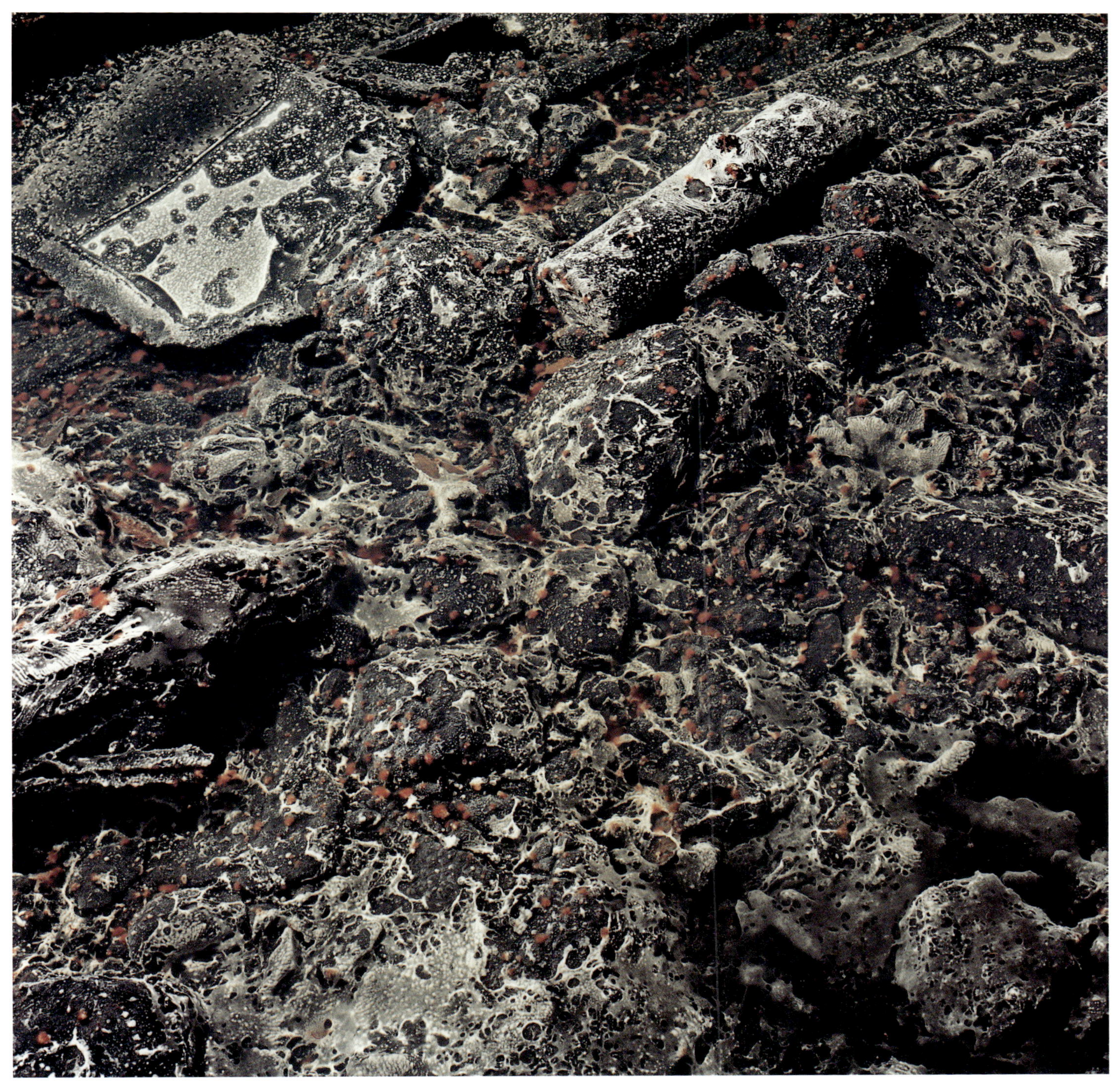

6011

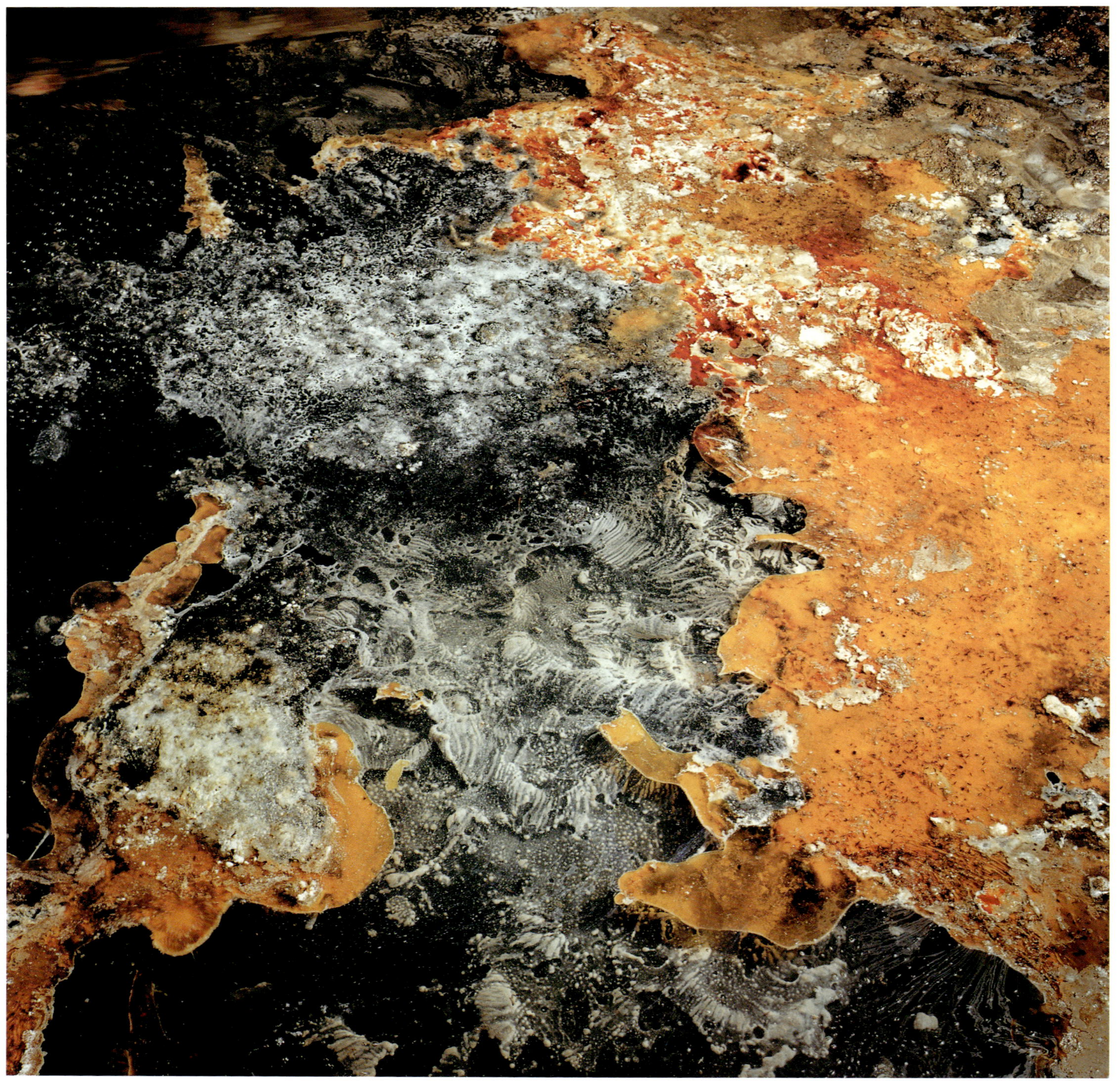

6202

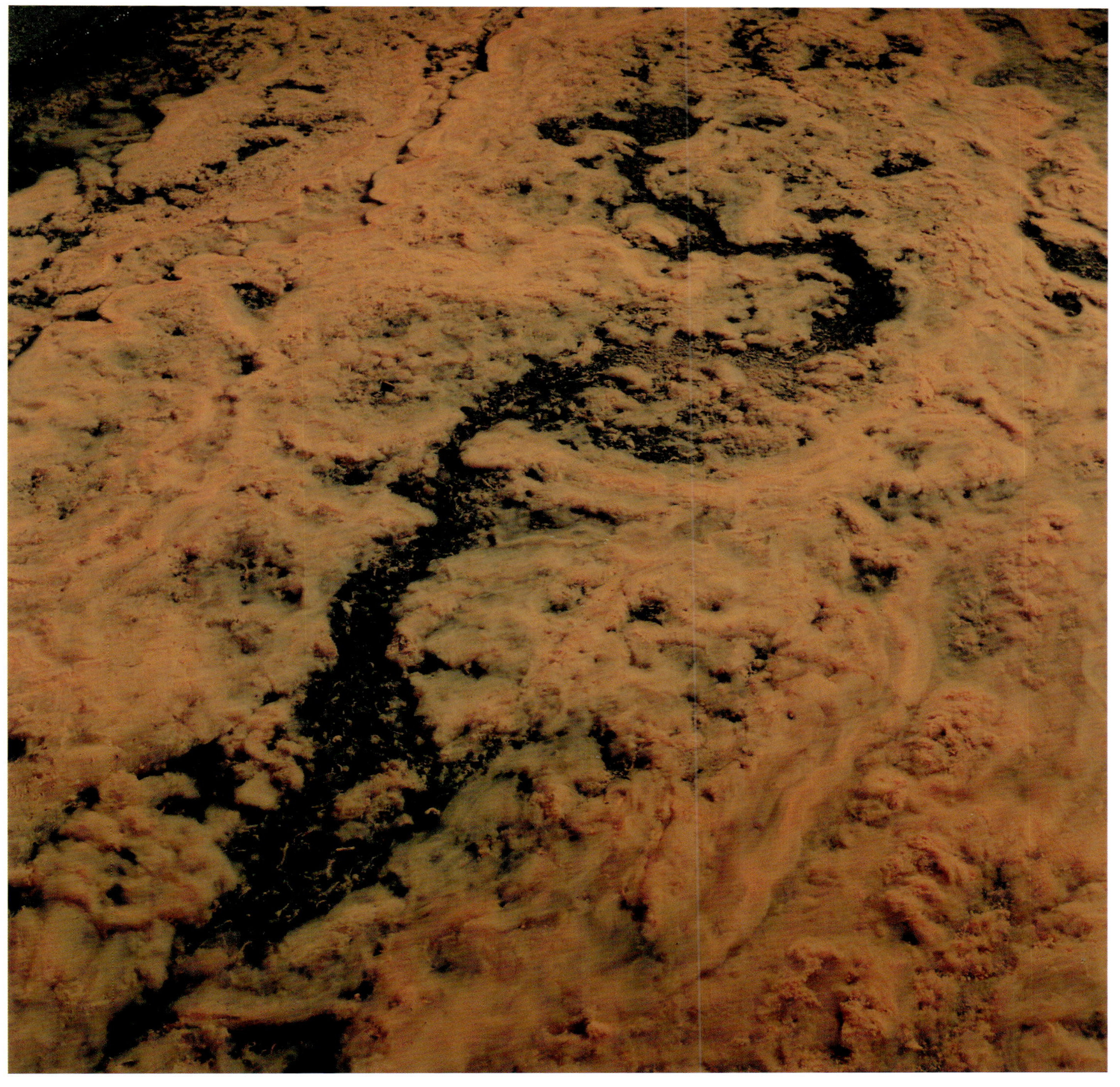

3108

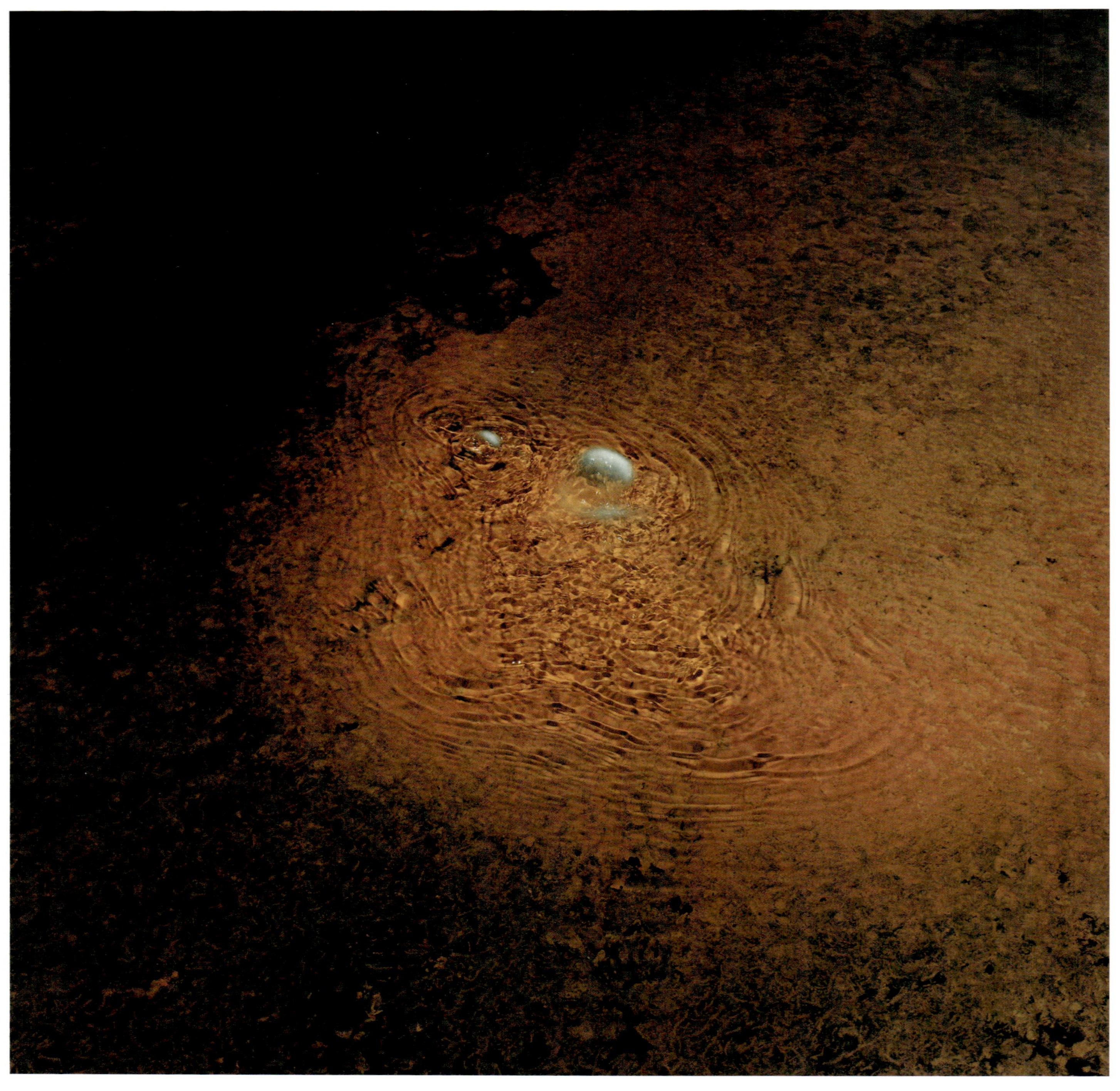

1502

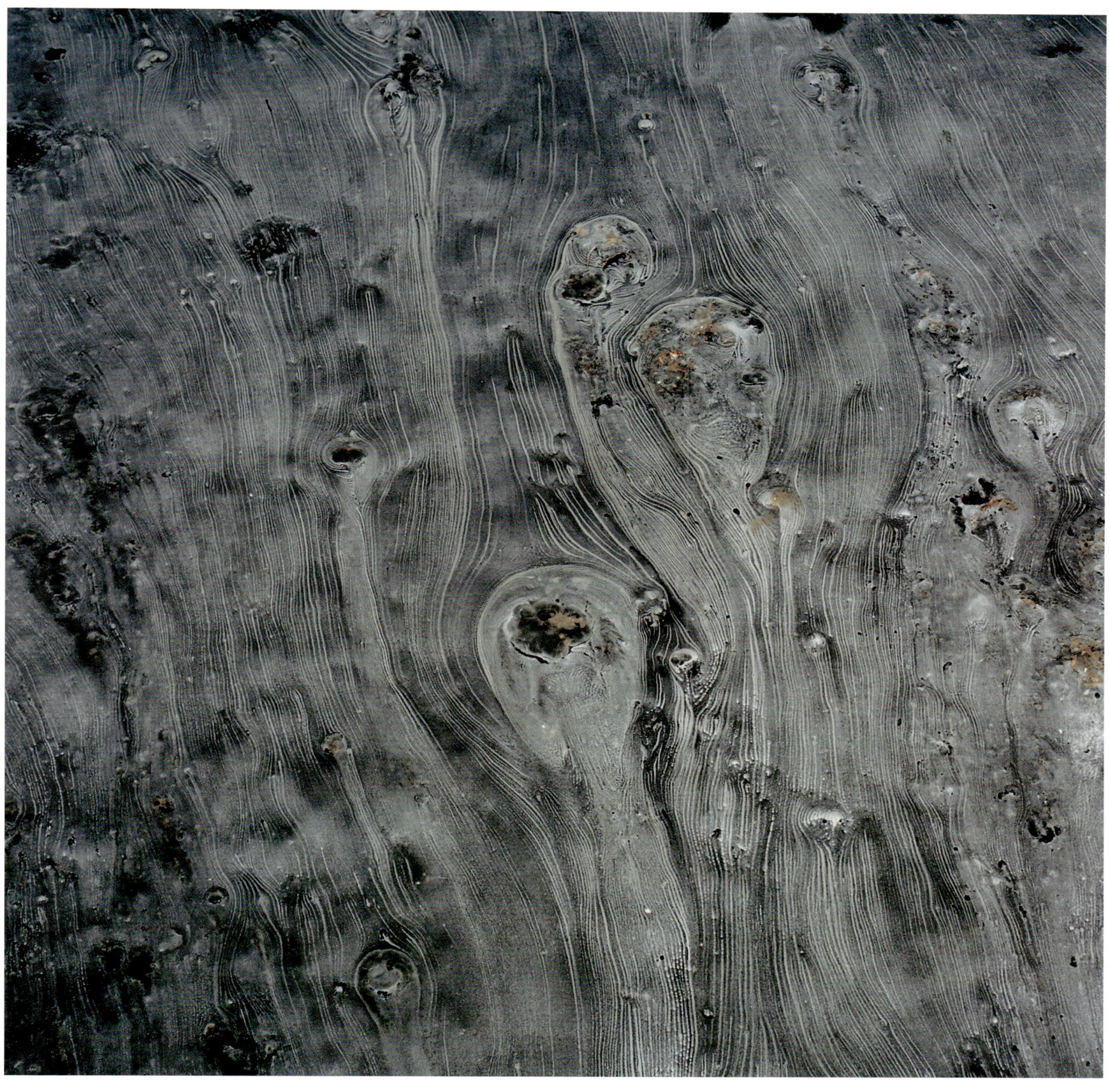

4809

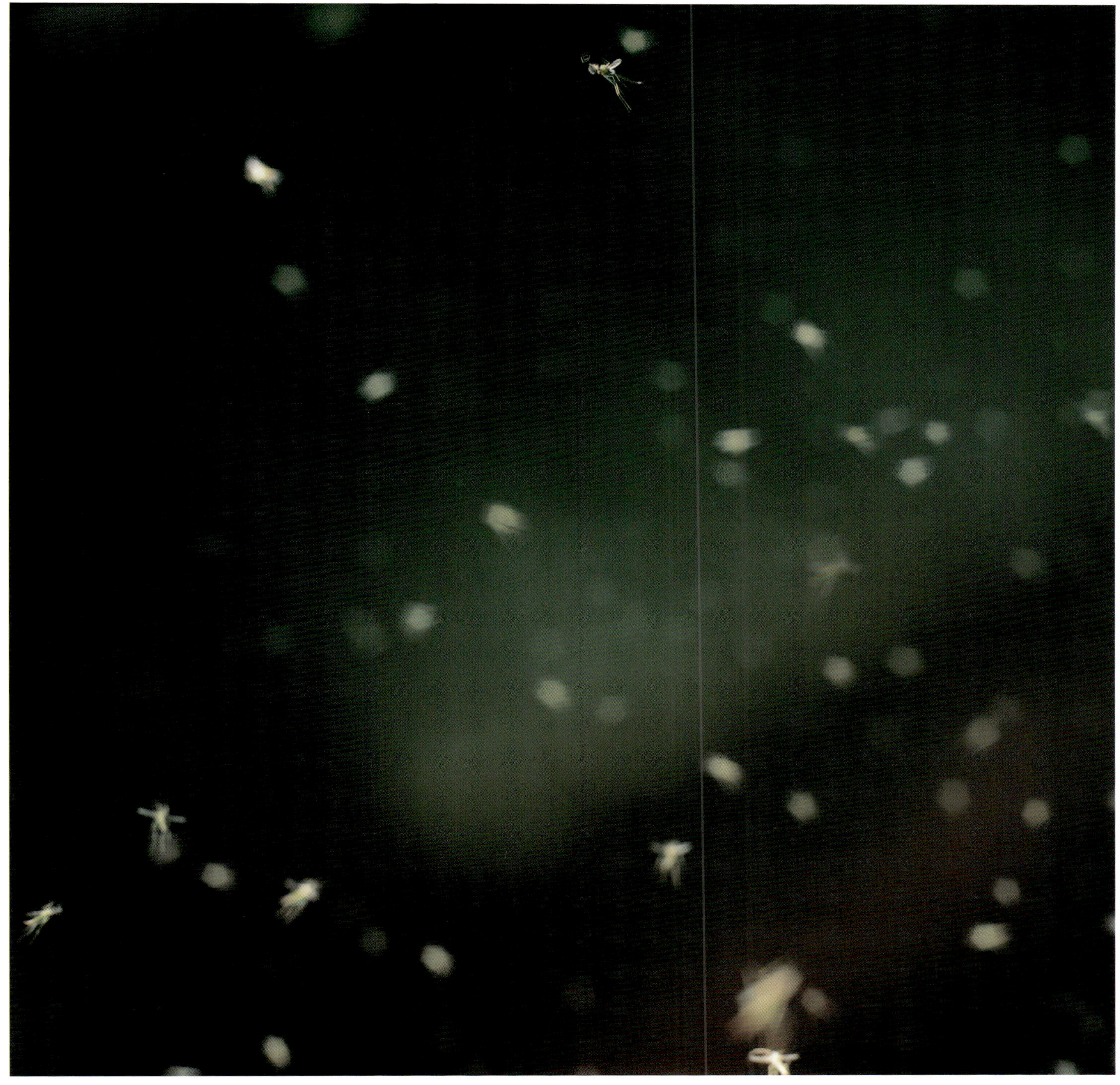

4505

Untitled

Untitled, 1989–97,
48 C-Prints, mounted on aluminum,
149 x 386 cm; 22.5 x 46 cm (each)
Courtesy Refco Group Ltd.

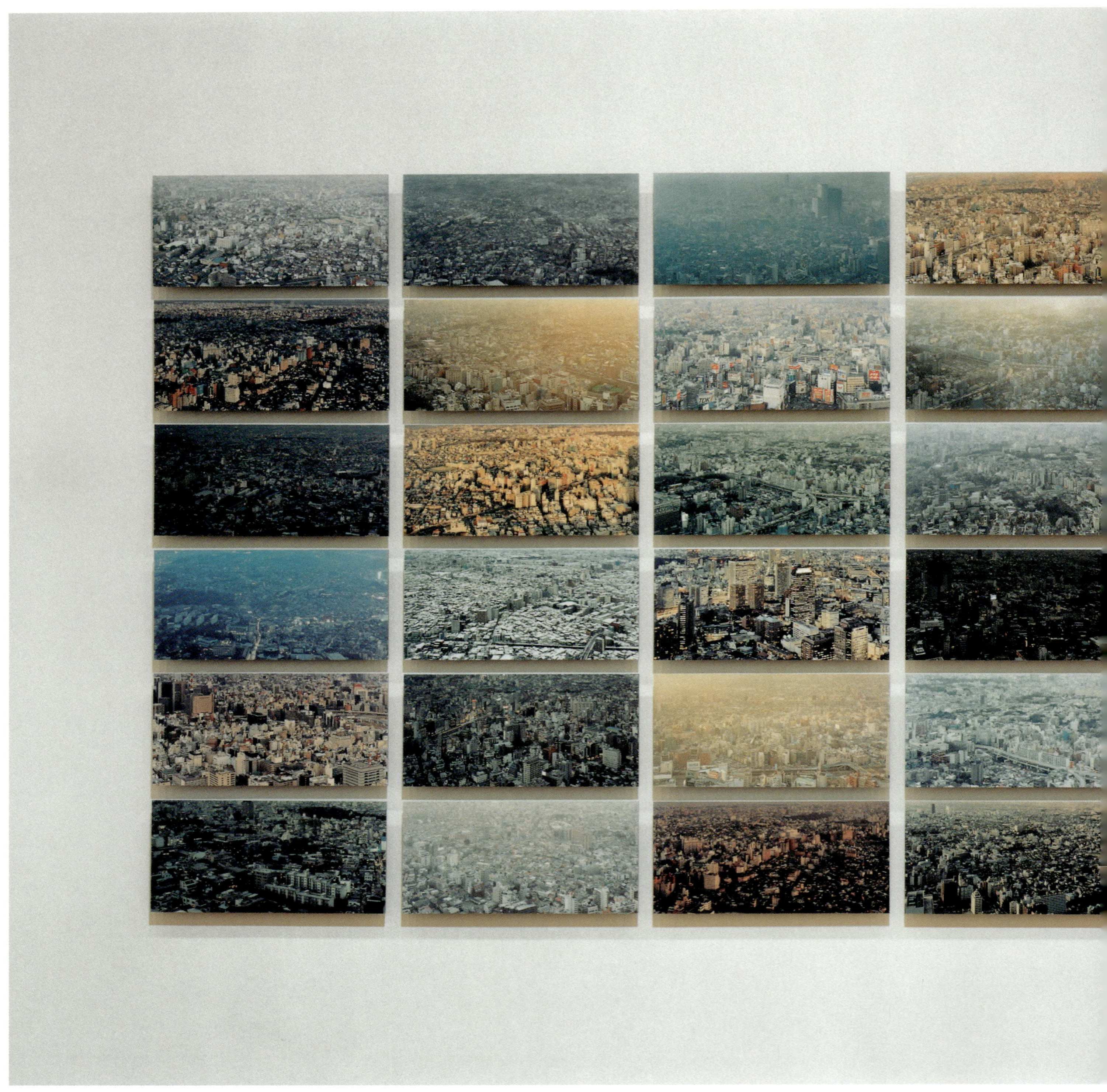

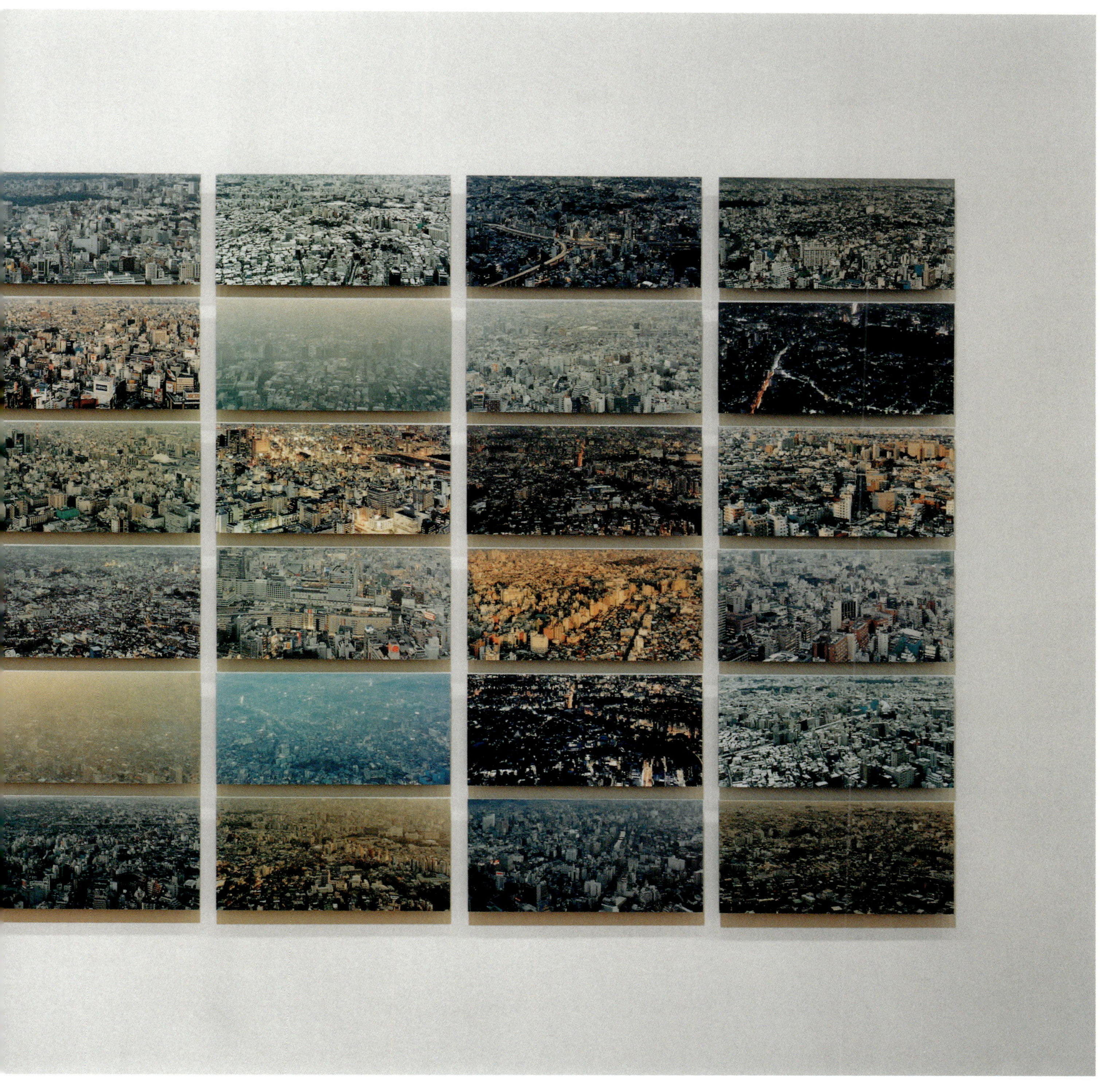

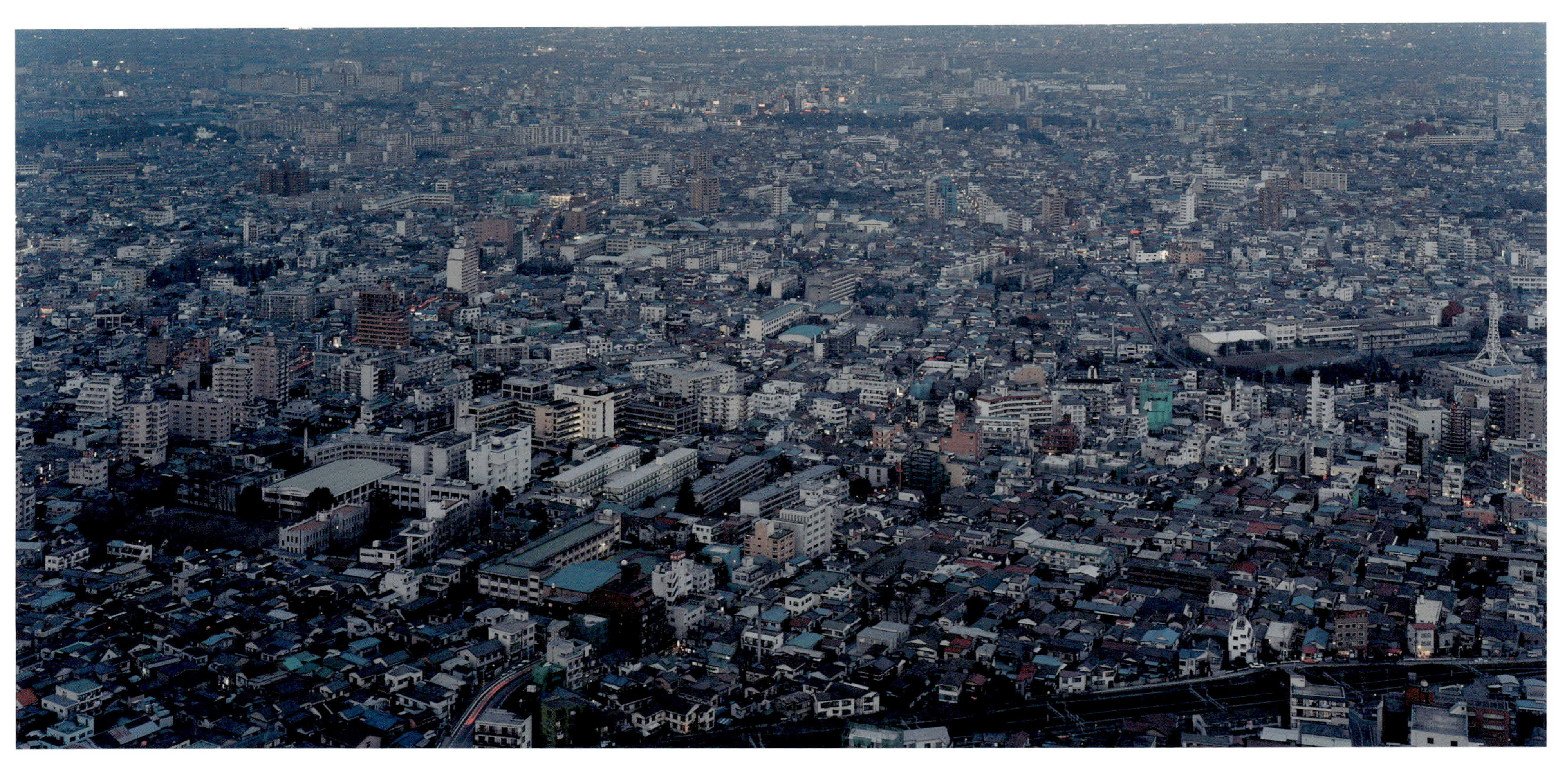

03917 1989

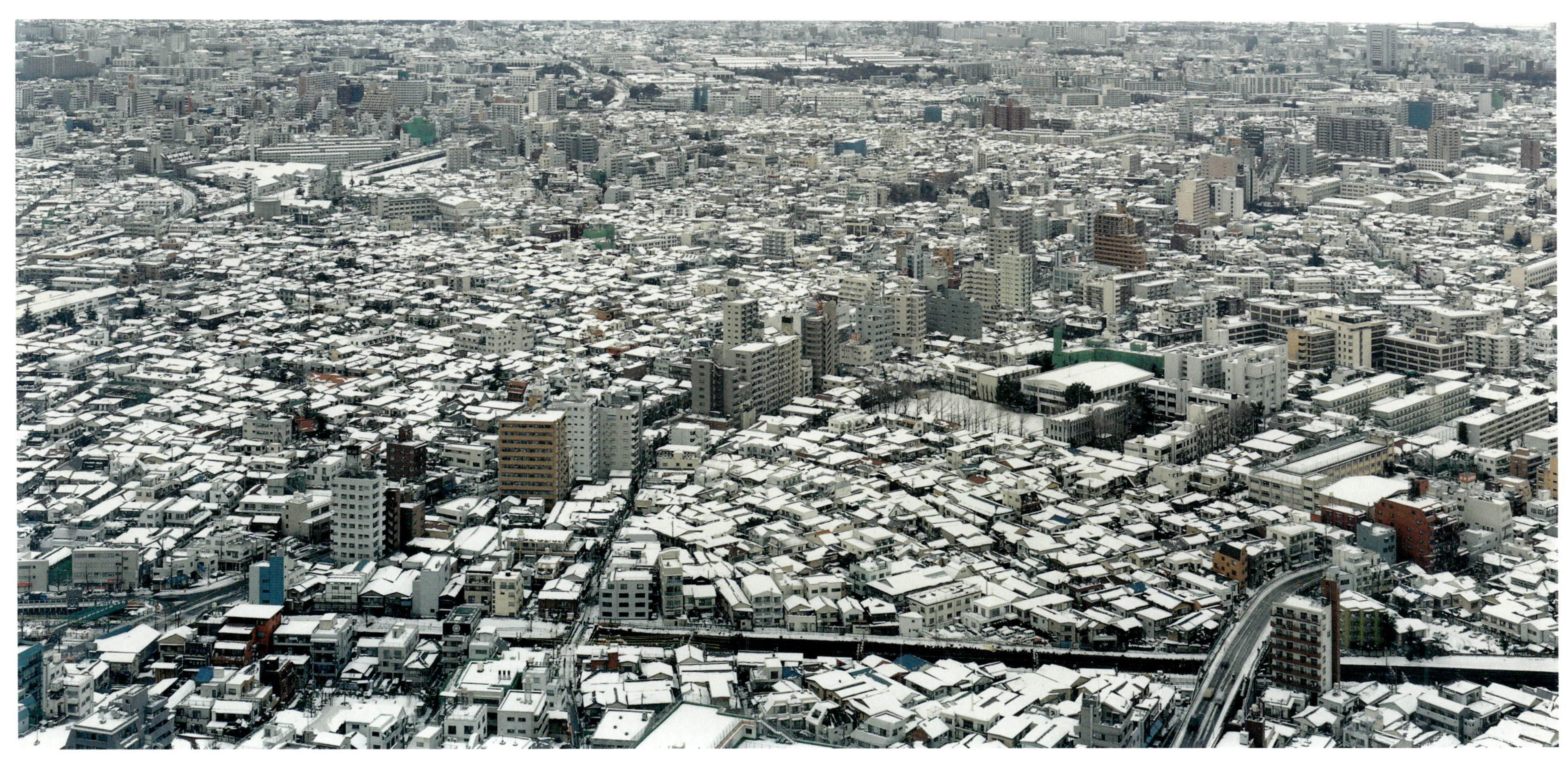

25305 1992

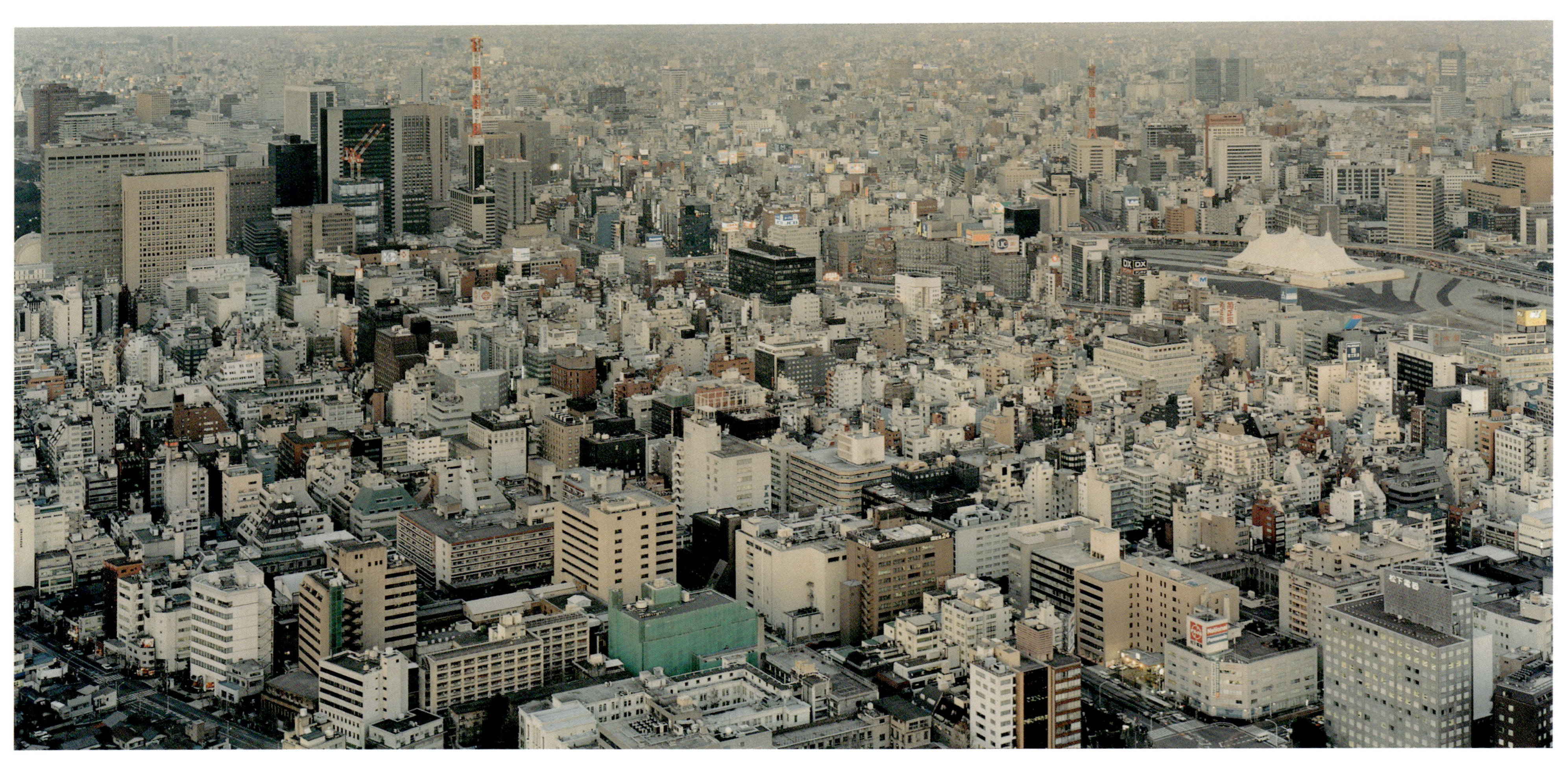

02708 1989

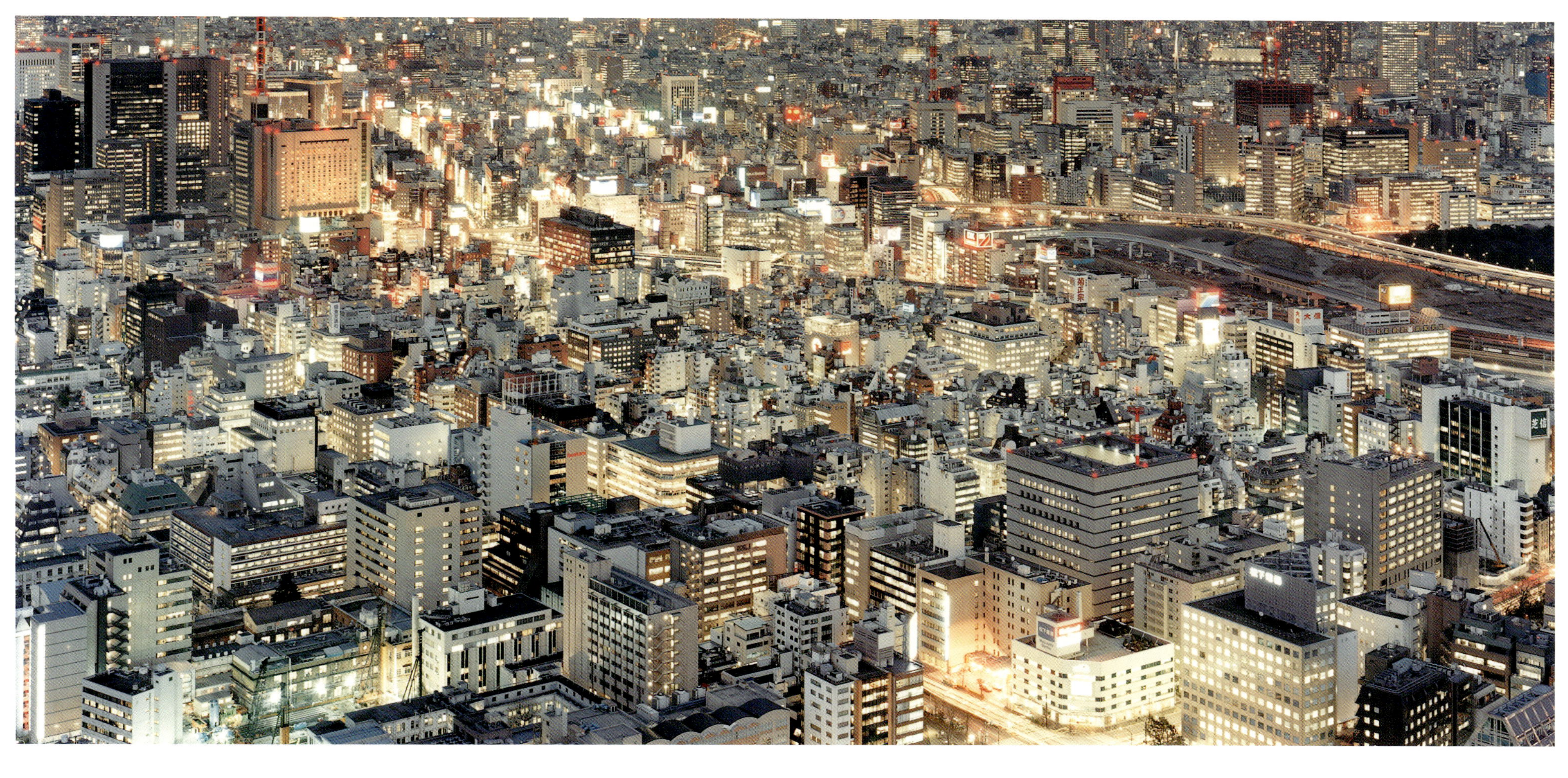

#52810 1997

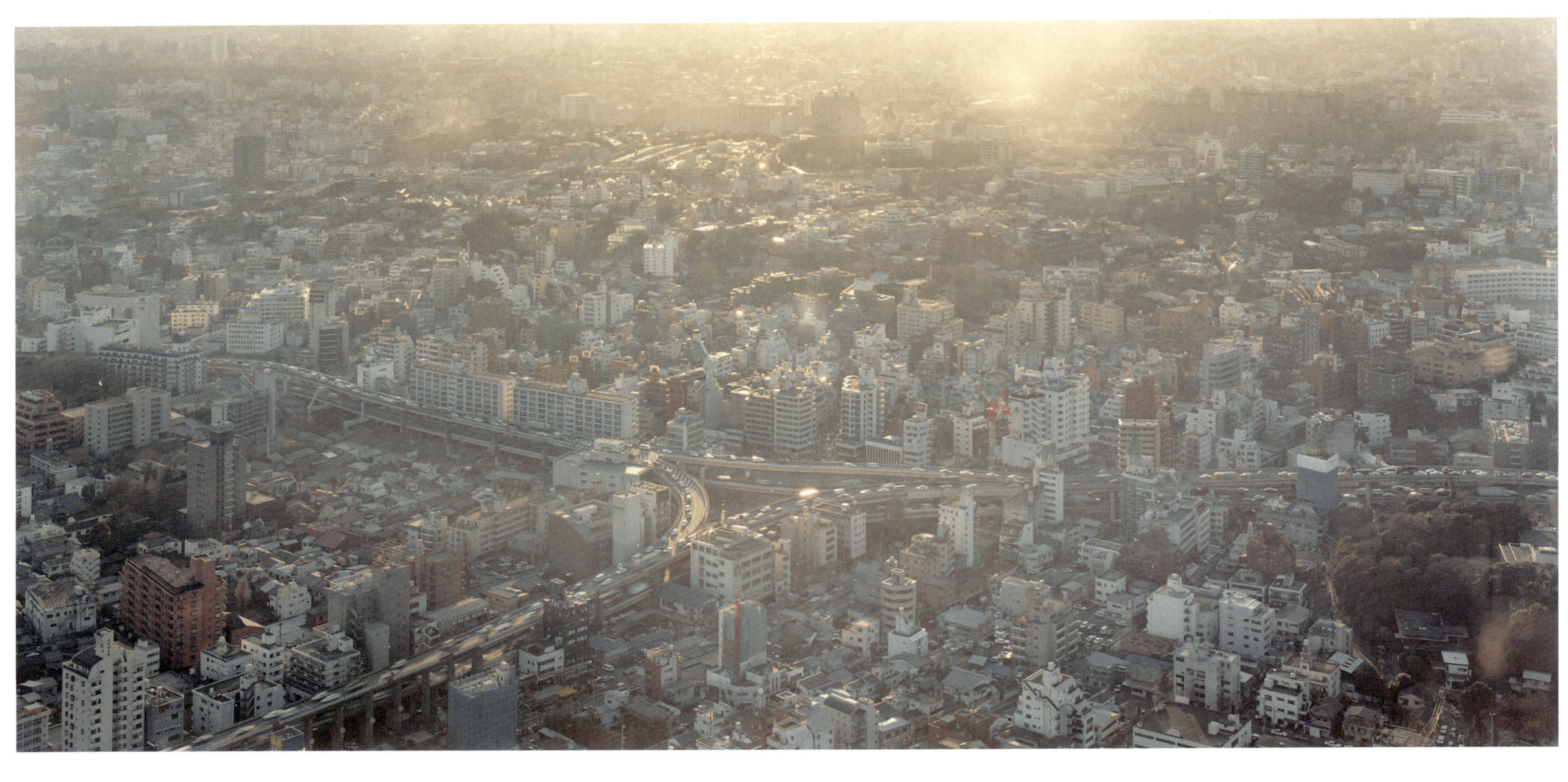

02411   1989

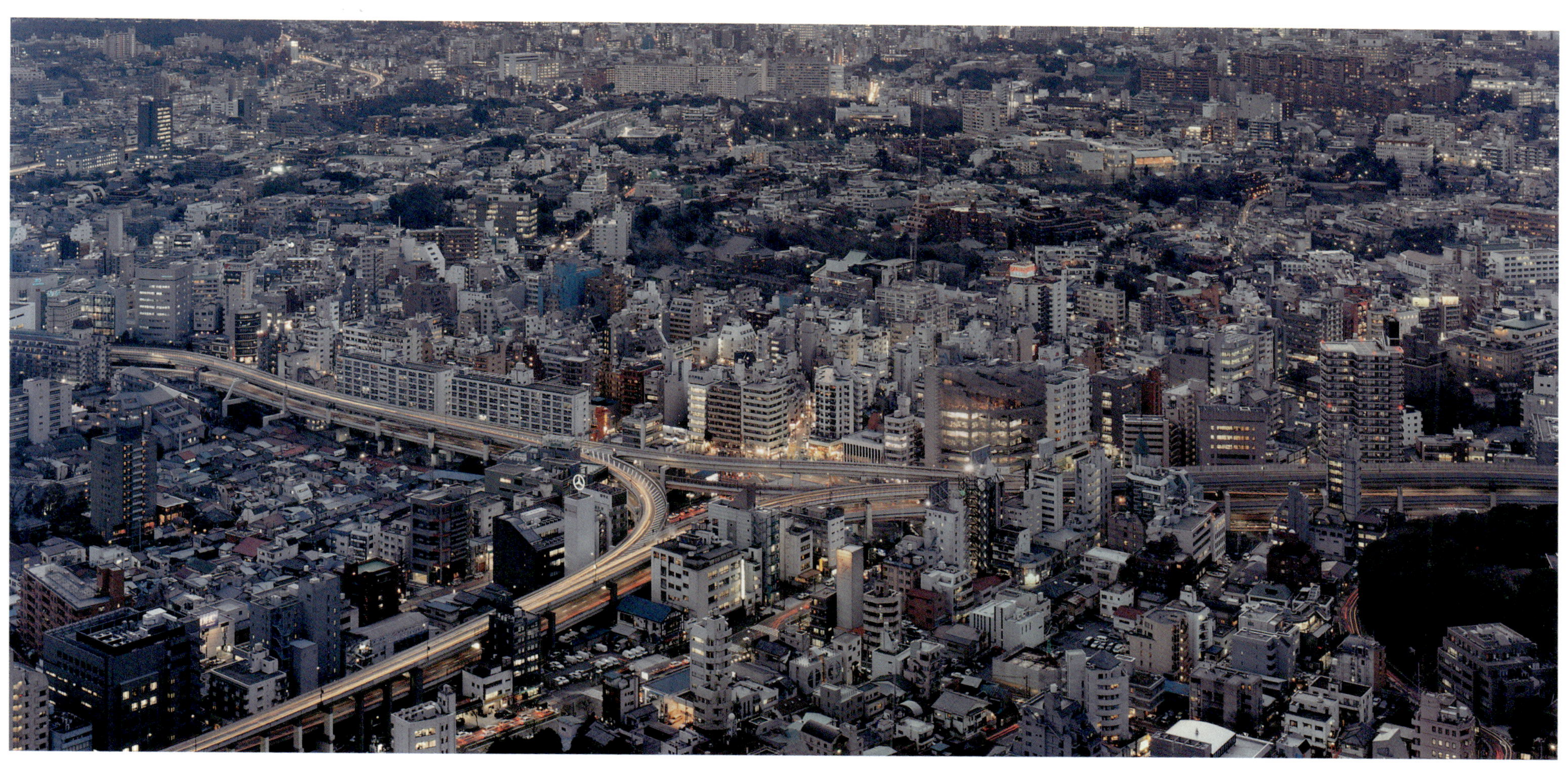

52716   1997

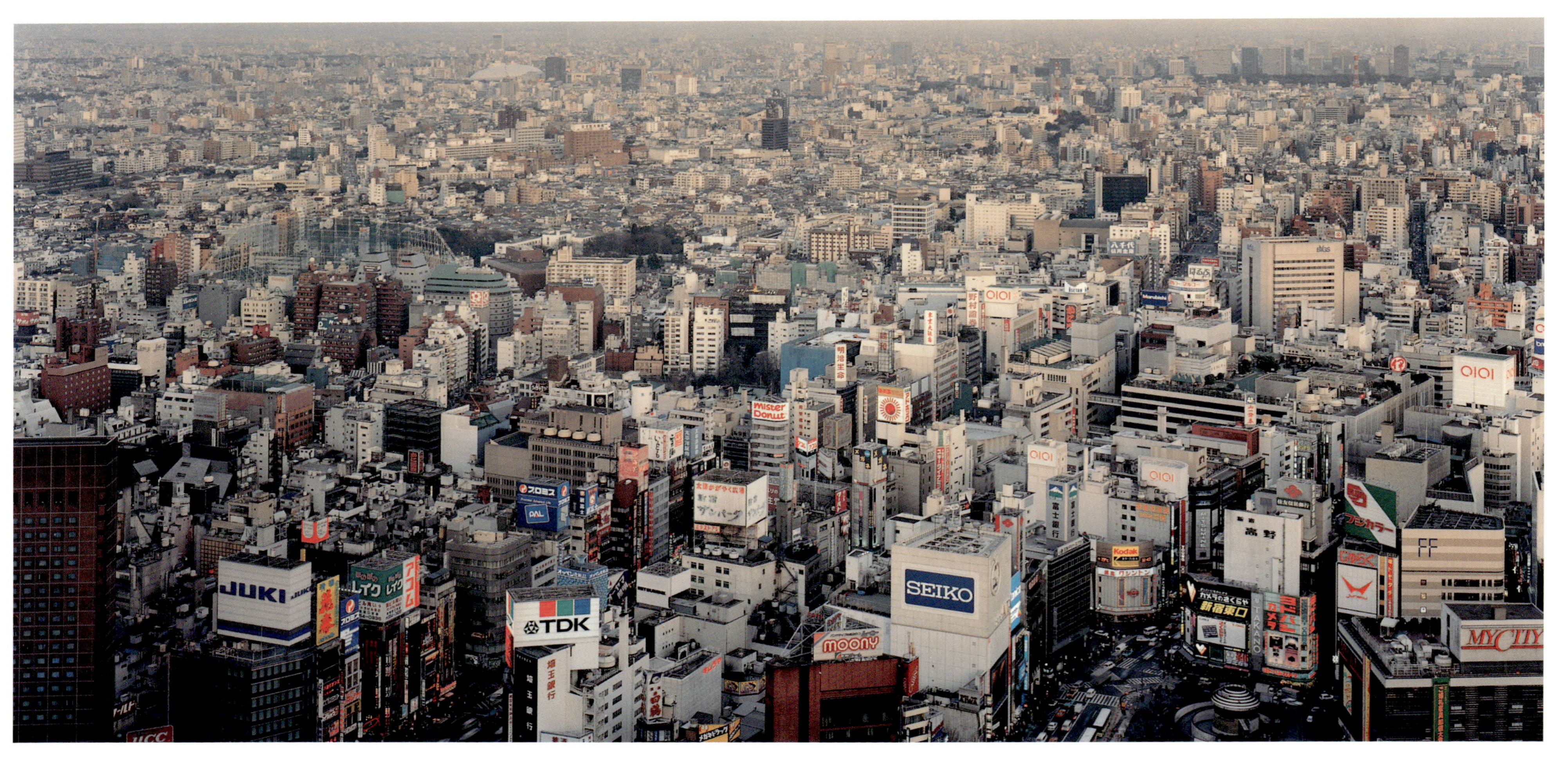

02005 1989

Panasonic
TDK!
MYCITY
メガネスーパー
さくらや
Konica
Asahi
ユニチャーム
住友カード
TBC
OIOI
mister Donut
brother
レイク

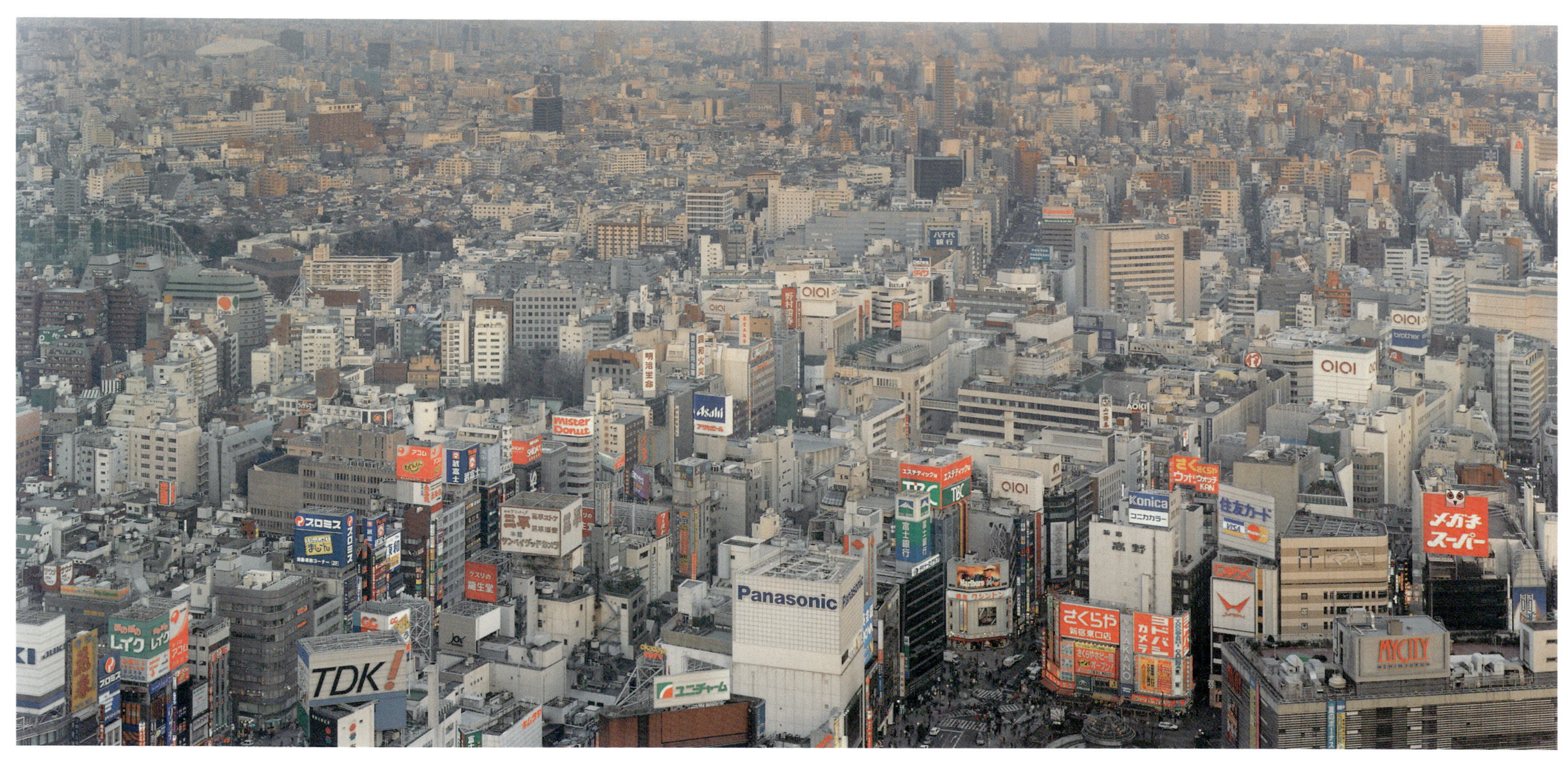

52107 1997

Untitled/Osaka

Untitled/Osaka, 1998–99,

2 C-Prints, mounted on aluminum, 89 x 180 cm (each)

Courtesy L.A. Galerie, Frankfurt on Main; the artist

毎日牛乳
Takashimaya
CITY
サンスター
お米はタワラ印
日産火災海上
サンケイスポーツ
大阪球場
学校法人 物療学園
大阪物療専門学校
0722-64-8663
アサヒビール
アイススケート
ボウリング
なんば大阪球場住宅博
ようこそ住宅博へ

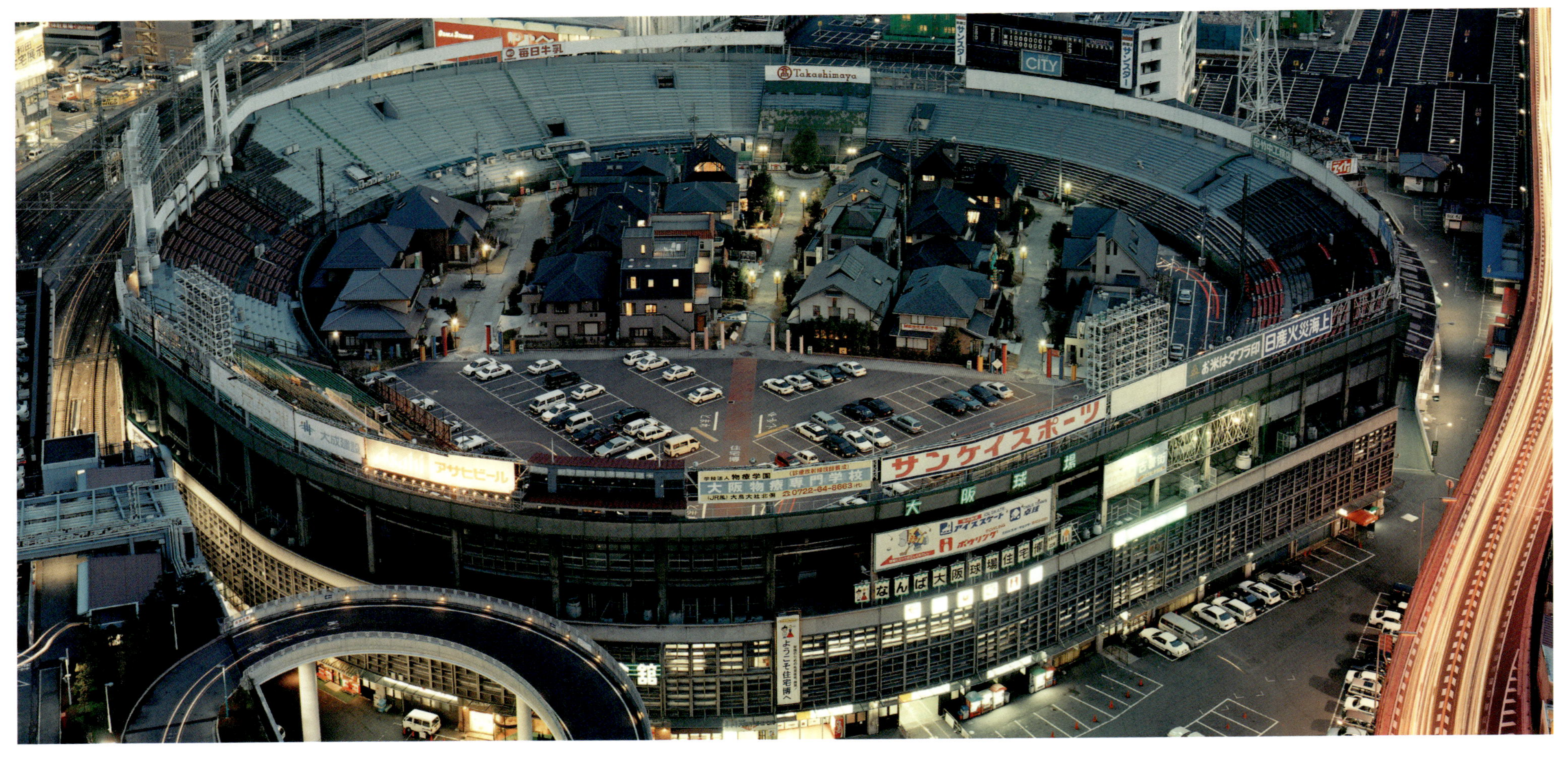

1998

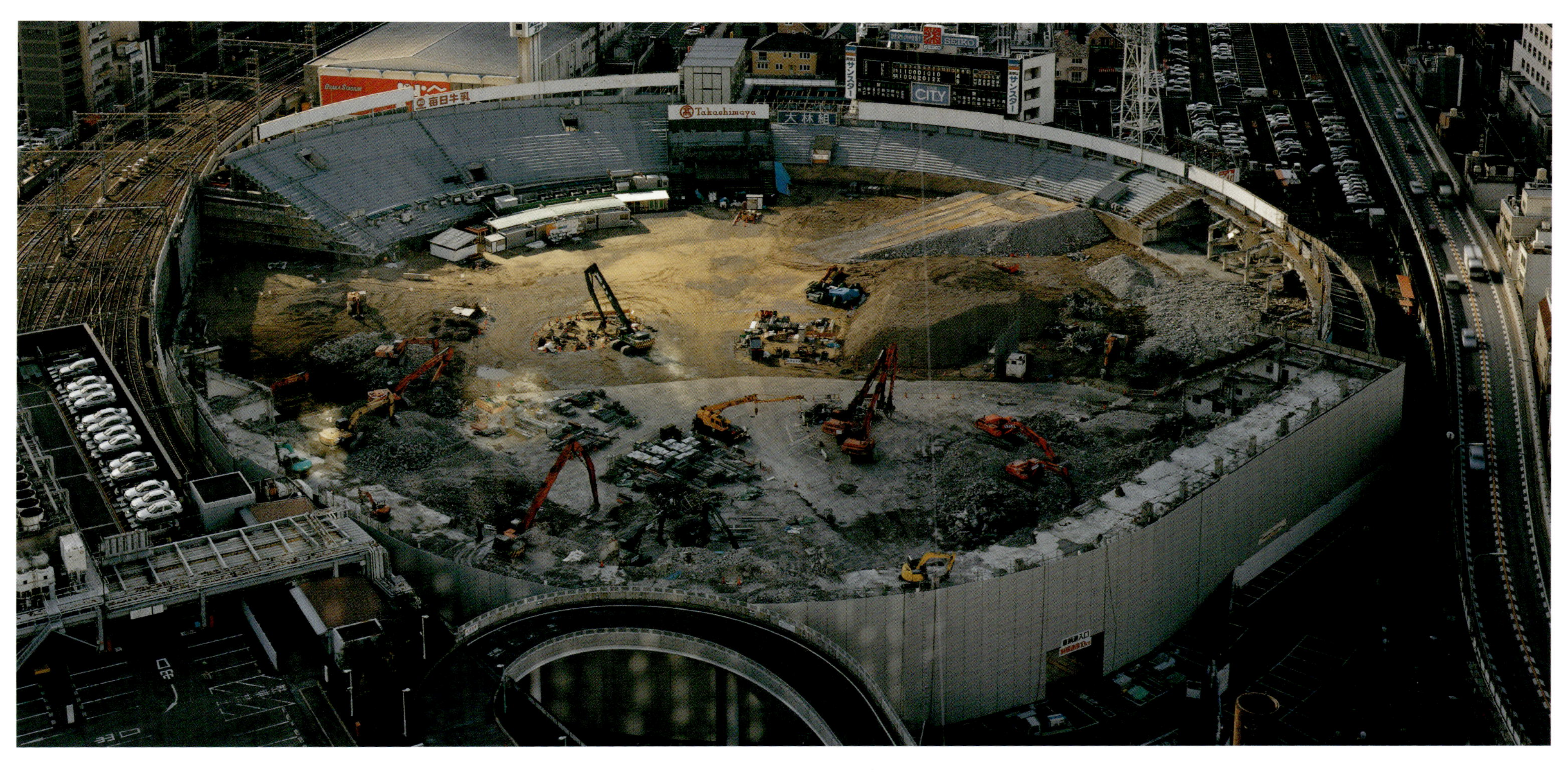

1999

Still Life

My Suzuki jeep is from Milton Keynes Council. Mr. Andrew Armes, the chief architect of Architecture MK, arranged it for me. I count myself fortunate to have it, because life is so hard without a car here in Milton Keynes. I am even more fortunate to have a key to the free petrol at the MK depot. Hey ho! My Suzuki has a big Milton Keynes Council logo on her black body; they use her only in the wintertime, which is why I may borrow her now for the spring.

When I am taking photographs on the housing estates, everybody asks me "What are you doing here?" Everybody is curious because I look odd: I am taking pictures of houses with an old-fashioned camera, a giant tripod, and a ladder, and I am wearing a fluorescent yellow waistcoat and a hat, and an Asian face.

"I am from Tokyo," I say. "I have been invited by the council to record developments in the town. Please look at the car: you can see the logo!"

They get friendly and start to chat:

"What are they planning to build in this empty plot? Do you know?"

"These houses have their own car park, but it's not big enough."

"I thought you were a surveyor."

Each house contains the life of a family. From the top of the ladder, the houses look so sweet.

They look like table-top models, like a still life. Still life? Why is life "still" in English? *Nature morte*, which means "dead nature," is the phrase the French use. *Seibutsu* is the Japanese which literally means "still object." To me still life sounds like "still alive" or "quiet life." And that reminds me of these people and their houses.

My Suzuki is in good condition. I get used to roundabouts, of course. Cool music from the radio, and nice colors from the sky. The car smells of the sweat of workmen inside.

Travelers hate the council logo and shout at me and throw water at the windscreen. But I am okay with her: car, camera, road, and houses; this is life in Milton Keynes.

Still Life, 2001, C-Print, 18.6 x 38 cm
Courtesy L.A. Galerie, Frankfurt on Main; the artist

Still Life

Mein Suzuki-Jeep gehört der Stadtverwaltung von Milton Keynes. Andrew Armes, der Chefarchitekt von Architecture MK, hat ihn mir besorgt. Ich bin glücklich, ihn zu haben, denn das Leben hier in Milton Keynes ist wirklich schwierig, wenn man kein Auto hat. Noch glücklicher bin ich über den Schlüssel, mit dem ich im städtischen Depot kostenlos tanken kann, hehe! Mein Suzuki hat ein großes Emblem der Stadt Milton Keynes auf seiner schwarz lackierten Karosserie. Er wird normalerweise nur im Winter benutzt, weshalb ich ihn jetzt für das Frühjahr ausleihen kann.

Wenn ich in den Neubaugebieten fotografiere, fragen alle: »Was machen Sie hier?« Alle sind neugierig, weil ich so merkwürdig aussehe: Ich fotografiere Häuser mit einer altmodischen Kamera, einem riesigen Stativ und einer Leiter; ich trage eine leuchtend gelbe Jacke und einen ebenso gelben Hut auf meinem asiatischen Kopf. – »Ich bin aus Tokio«, sage ich. »Ich wurde von der Stadtverwaltung eingeladen, um die Entwicklung der Stadt zu dokumentieren. Hier steht mein Auto, sehen Sie das Emblem der Stadtverwaltung.« – Dann werden sie freundlich und fangen an zu reden: »Was soll auf diesem leeren Grundstück gebaut werden? Wissen Sie das?« – »Diese Häuser haben ihre eigenen Garagen und Parkplätze, aber die reichen nicht aus.« – »Ich dachte zuerst, Sie wären ein Vermesser.«

Jedes Haus birgt das Leben einer Familie. Von oben auf der Leiter sehen die Häuser so reizend aus. Wie Modelle, wie ein Stillleben. Stillleben? Warum ist dieses Leben »still«? Die Franzosen sagen »nature morte«, tote Natur. Das japanische Wort ist »seibutsu«, was wörtlich übersetzt »ruhender Gegenstand« bedeutet. Für mich klingt »Stillleben« wie »noch am Leben« oder »stilles Leben«. Und das erinnert mich an die Leute und ihre Häuser.

Mein Suzuki fährt gut. Allmählich gewöhne ich mich an den Kreisverkehr. Nette Musik im Radio und die hübschen Farben des Himmels. Im Inneren riecht das Auto nach dem Schweiß von Arbeitern.

Die Landfahrer hassen das städtische Emblem auf meinem Auto, sie schreien mich an und spritzen Wasser auf die Windschutzscheibe. Aber mir soll's recht sein: Auto, Kamera, Straßen und Häuser – so ist das Leben in Milton Keynes.

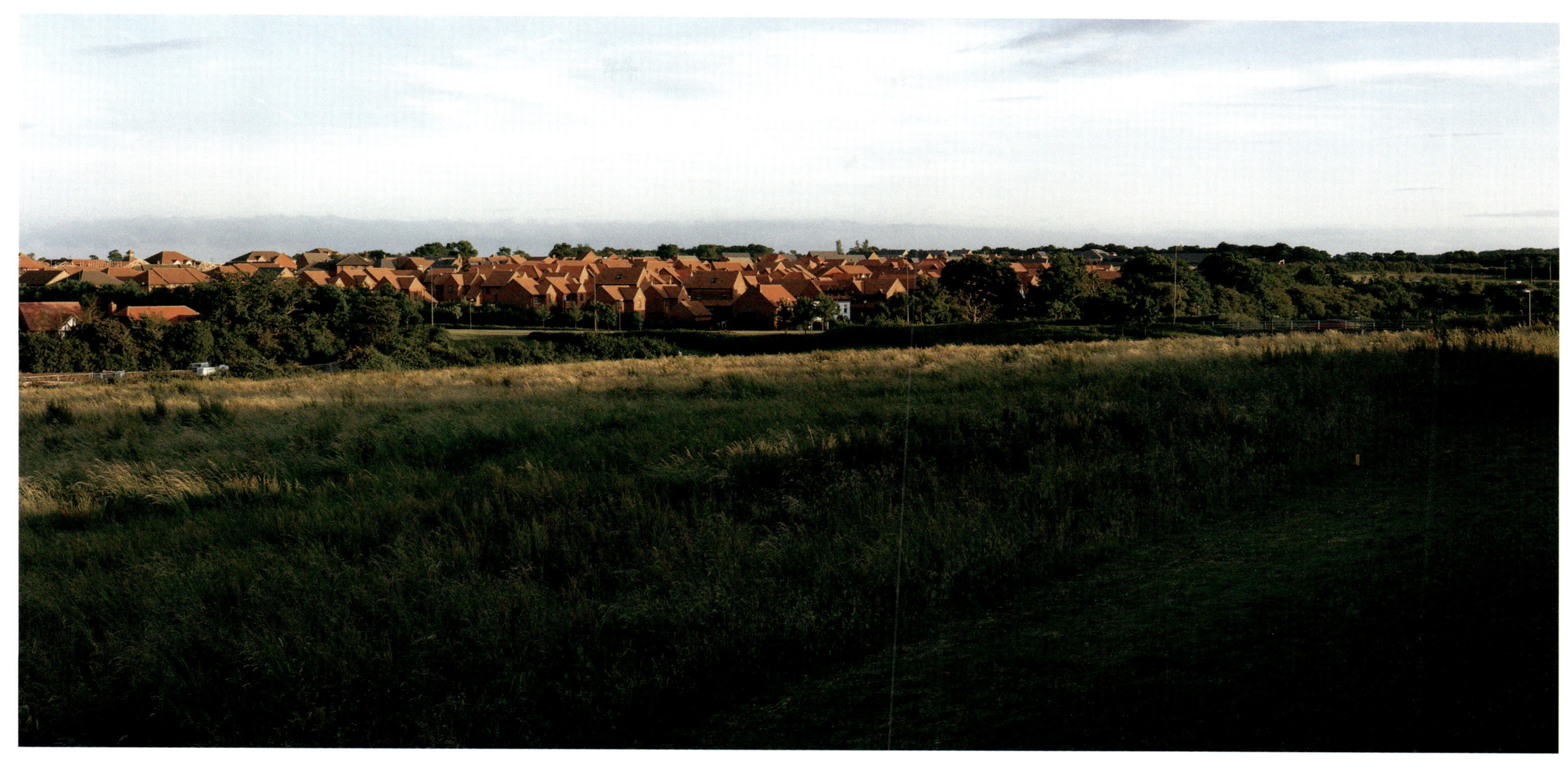

044

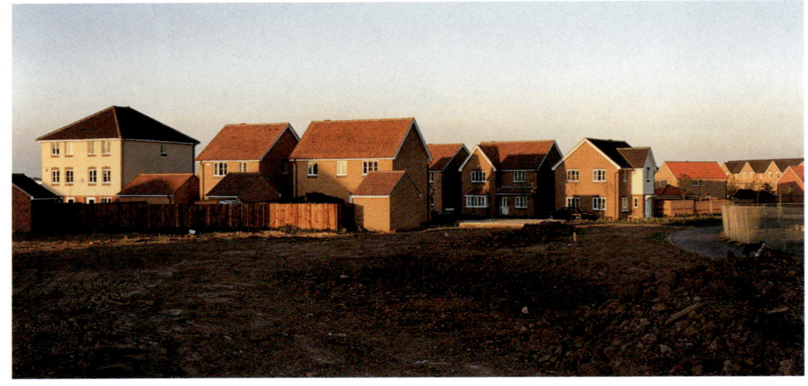

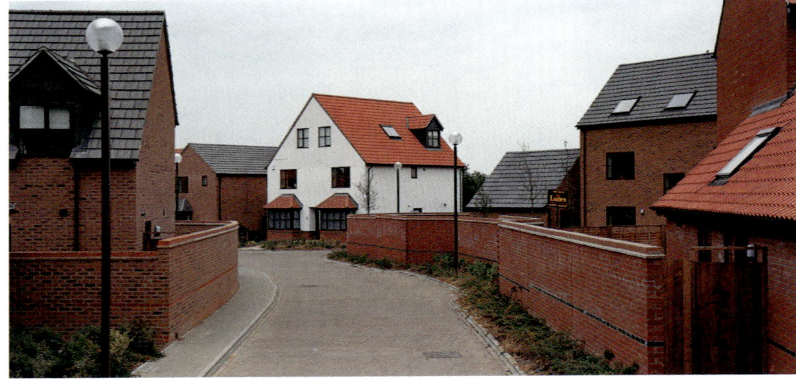

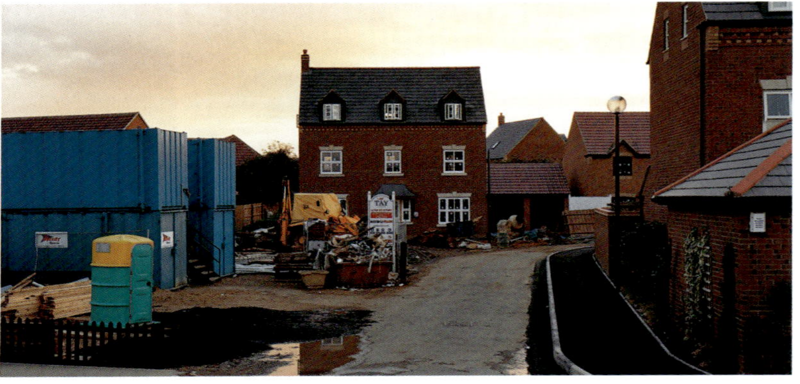

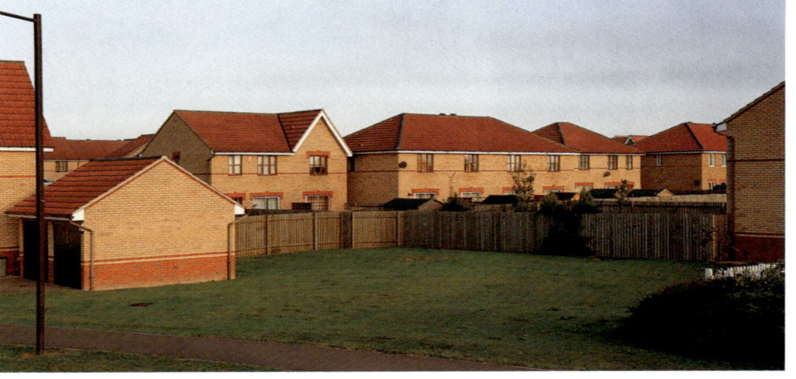

031 # 066 # 088 # 102

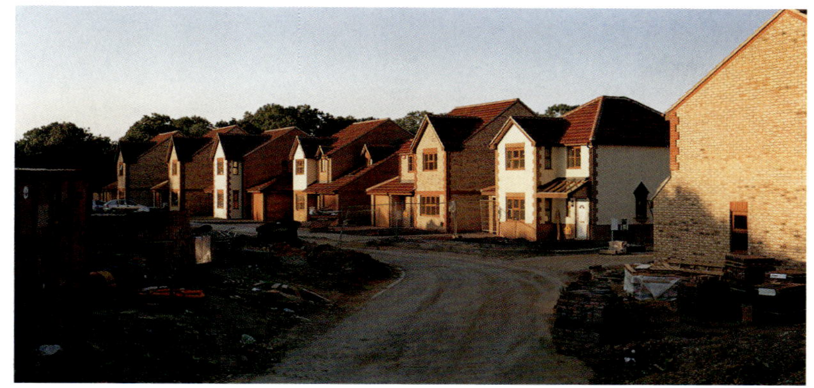

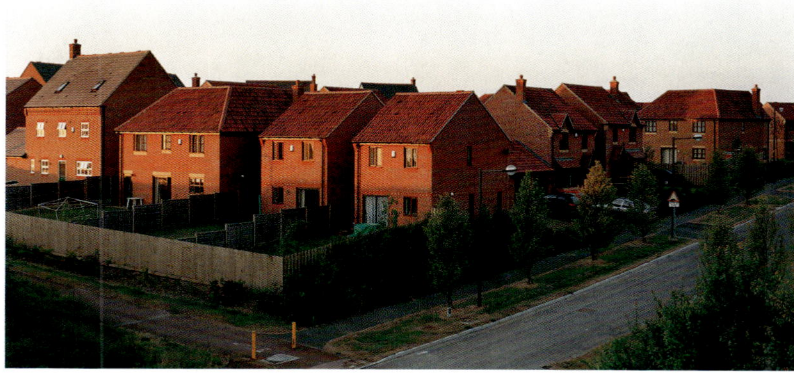

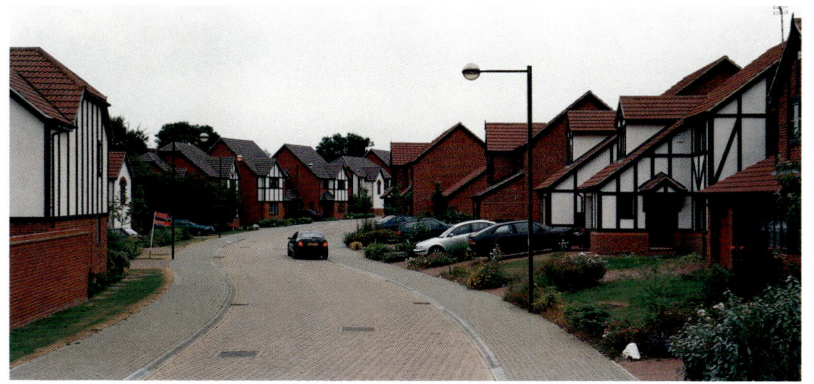

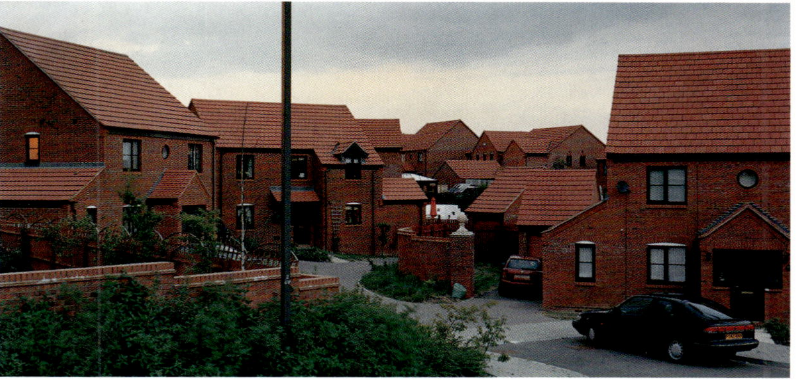

003 # 059 # 071 # 108

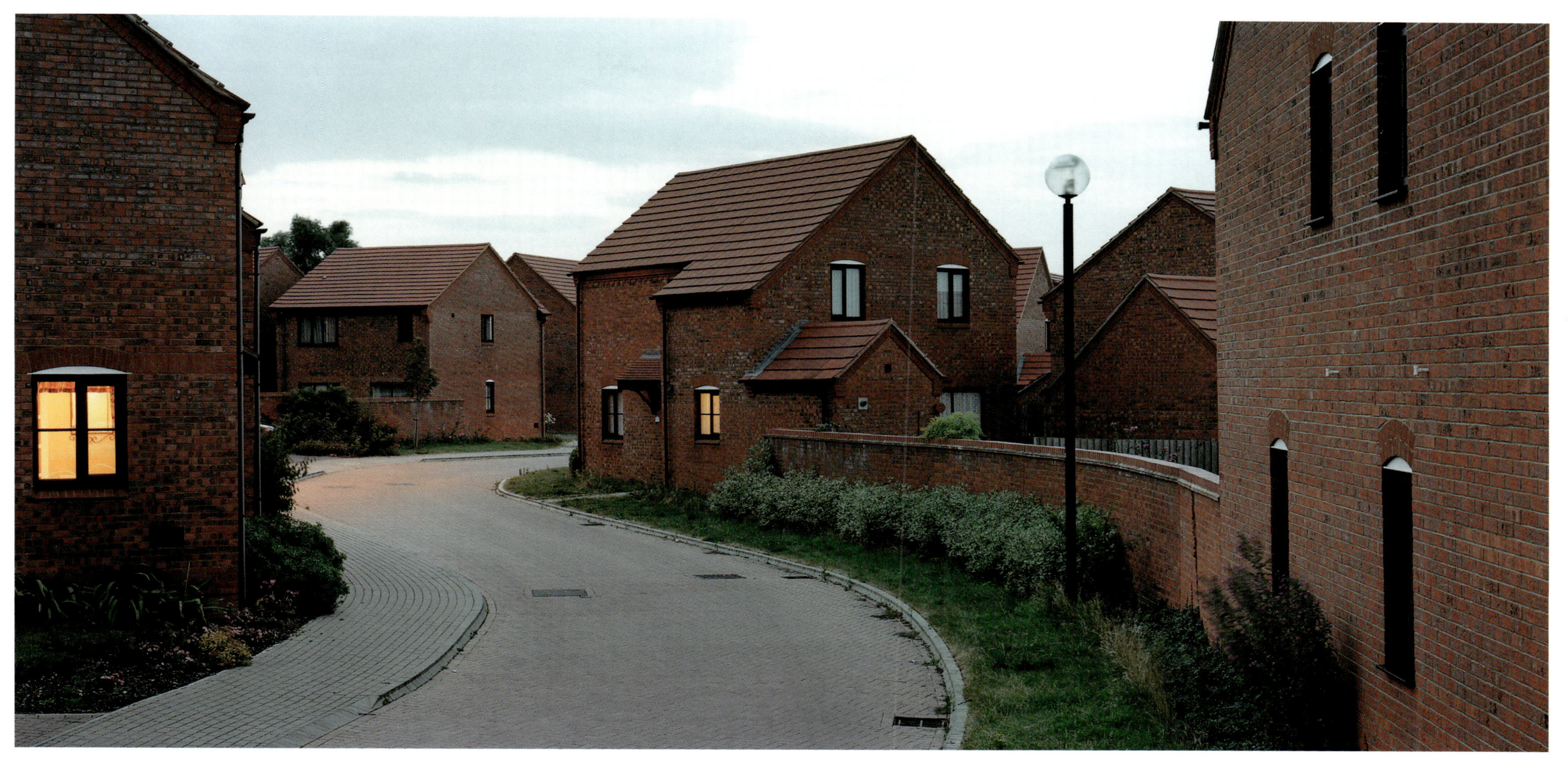

109

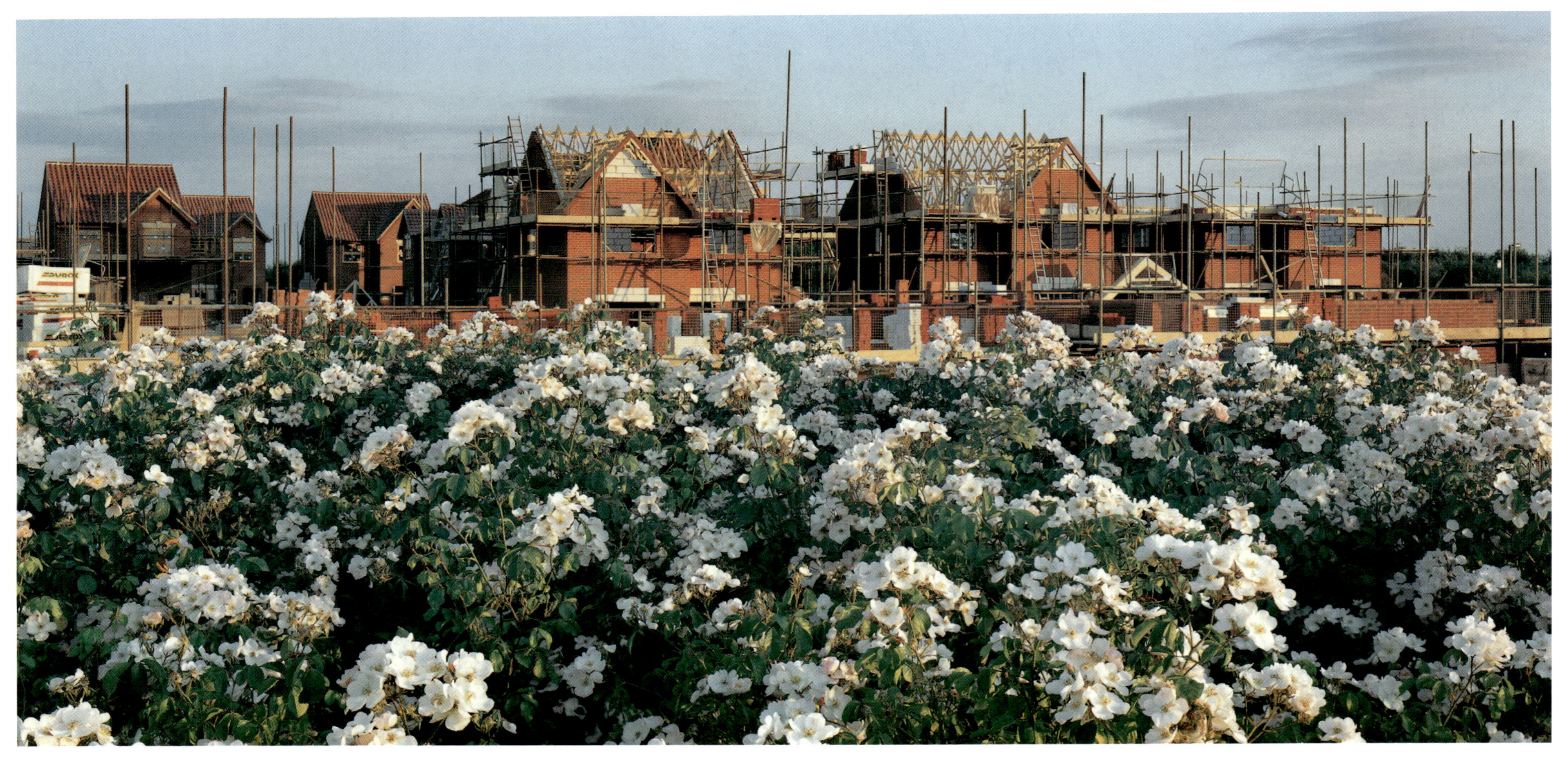

056

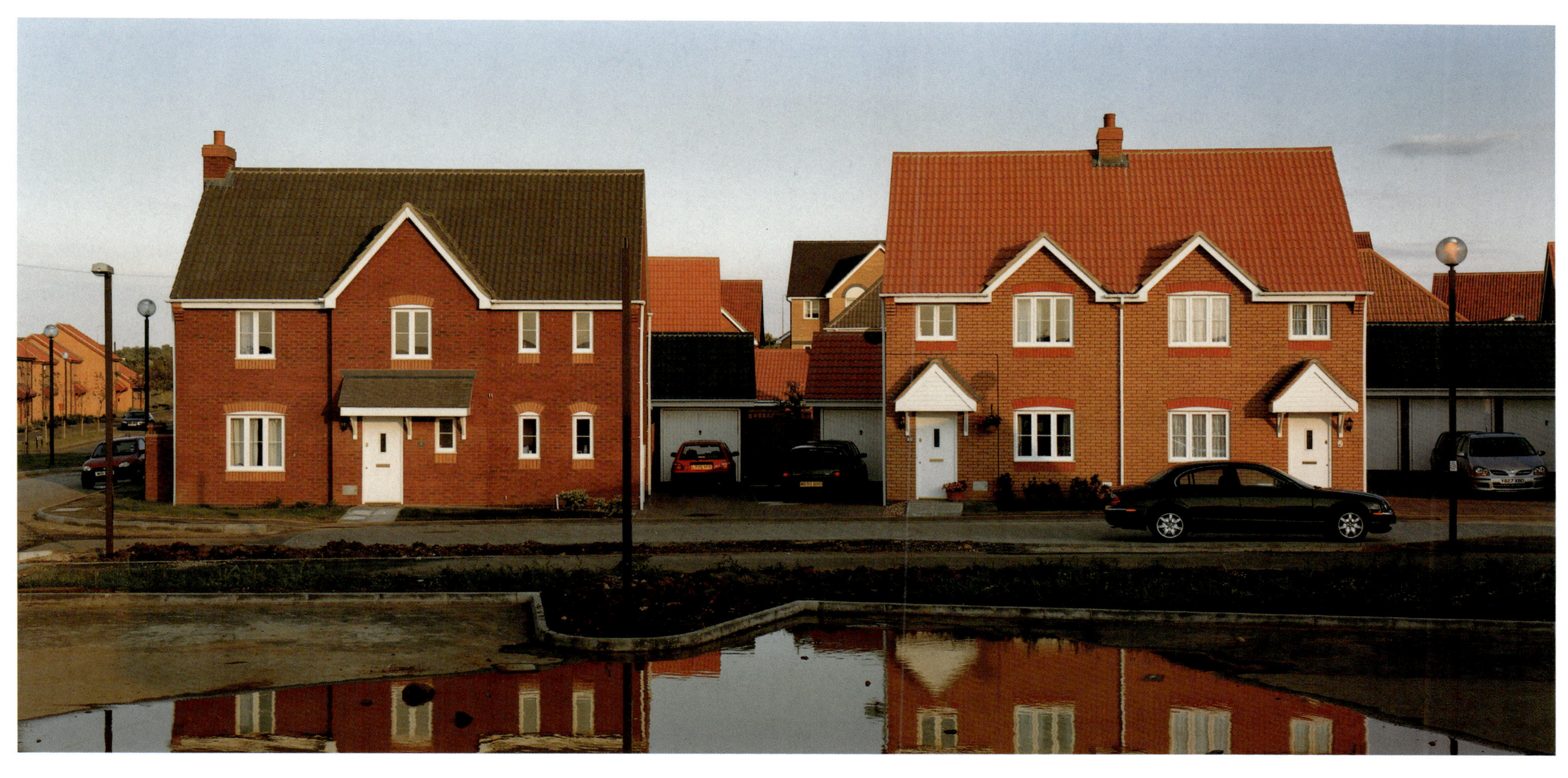

083

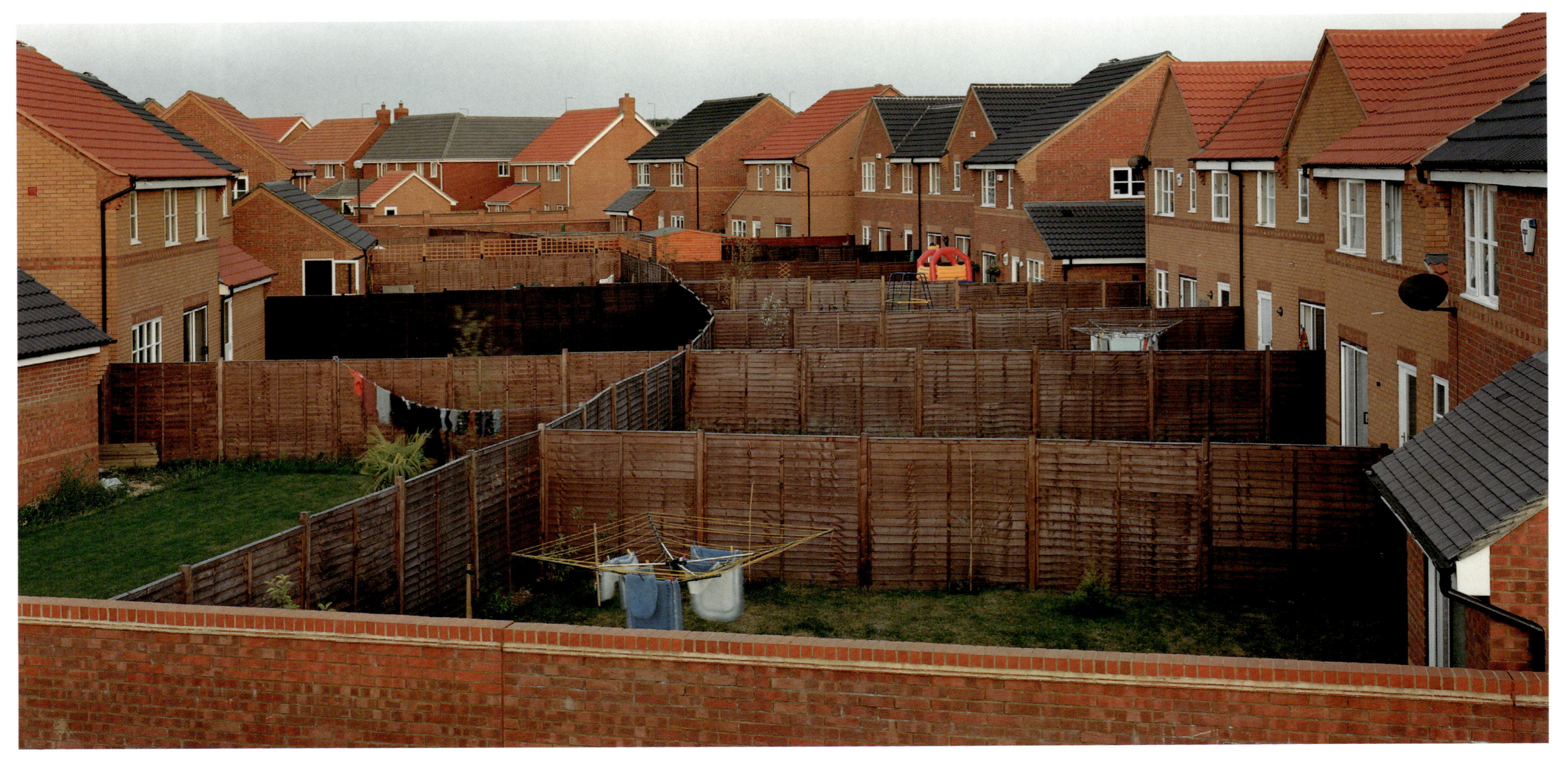

039

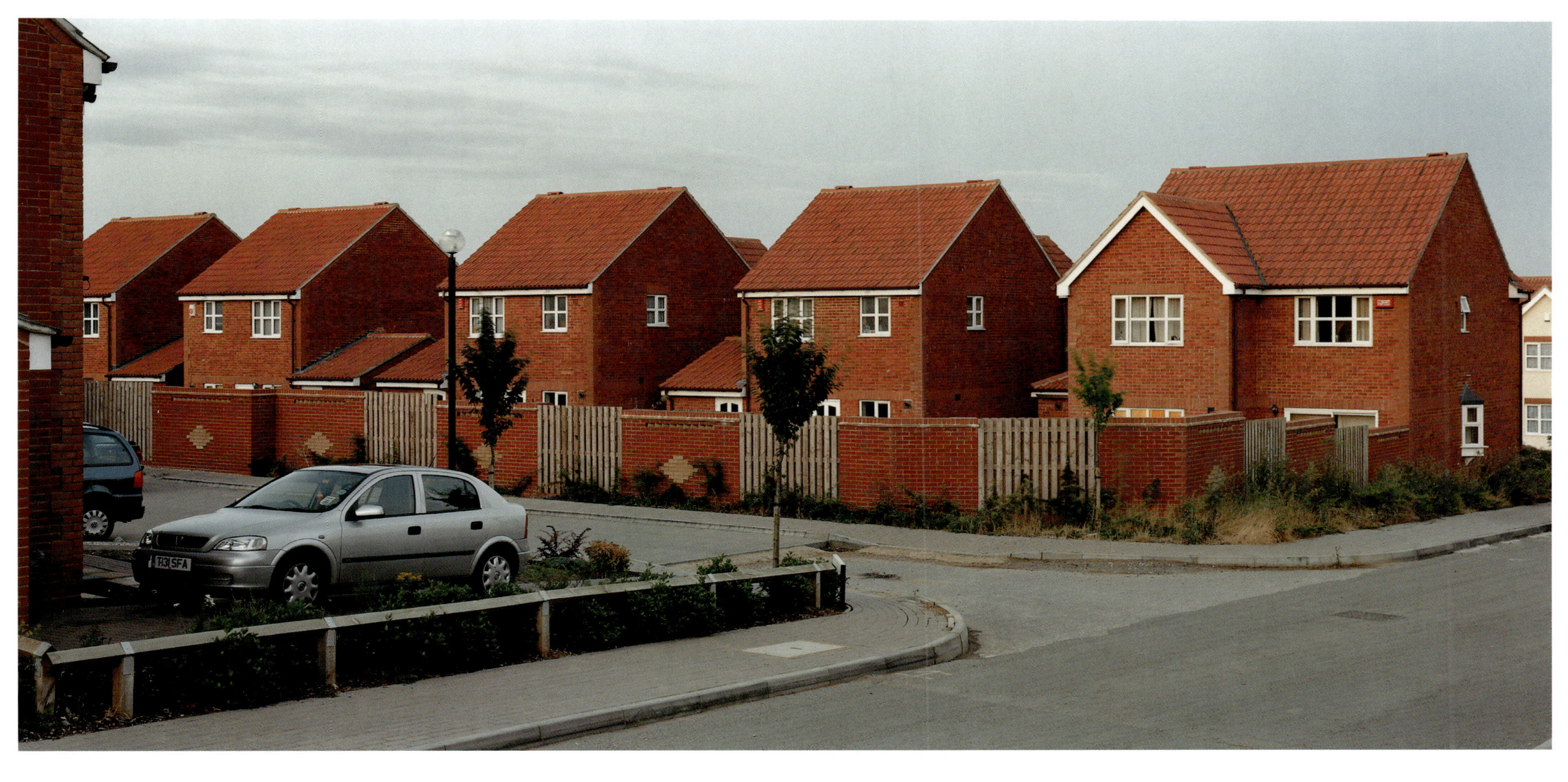

079

Slow Glass

In the science fiction of Bob Shaw, there is an invention called Slow Glass which slows the speed of light. When you look into the glass you can see a scene from the past. So the story goes, with Slow Glass you can enjoy a beautiful landscape which has been stored in it, in the privacy of your city apartment. A piece of broken Slow Glass which has recorded a crime may be used as evidence in court.

But it seems to me that within our sophisticated society this kind of function is already realized in a wide variety of recording methods.

The story goes on to tell of the misery that is caused when the past invades someone's mind as a persistent memory. This is also a familiar experience in modern life because all our memories are stored for us in technological media and not in our minds. The enormous quantity of this material makes us uneasy.

Our age is illuminated by all kinds of light from the past which shines into the darkest corners. It is like an interior architectural space completely glazed in Slow Glass. There is no shade; everything is cruelly bright.

Slow Glass, 2001, C-Print, mounted on aluminum, 90 x 120 cm
Courtesy L.A. Galerie, Frankfurt on Main; the artist

Slow Glass

In Bob Shaws Science-fiction-Erzählungen gibt es eine Erfindung mit dem Namen »Slow Glass« – langsames Glas –, ein Material, das die Geschwindigkeit des Lichts verringert. Wenn man in das Glas schaut, sieht man Szenen aus der Vergangenheit. So kann man mit »Slow Glass« eine schöne Landschaft betrachten, die darin gespeichert ist, und dabei die ganze Zeit in seiner Großstadtwohnung bleiben. Eine Scherbe dieses Glases, in der ein Verbrechen aufgezeichnet ist, kann in einer Gerichtsverhandlung als Beweismittel verwendet werden.

Aber mir scheint, dass unsere hoch entwickelte Gesellschaft diese Funktion schon in einer Vielzahl anderer Aufzeichnungstechniken verwirklicht hat.

Die Geschichte erzählt aber auch davon, welches Unglück entstehen kann, wenn die Vergangenheit sich als unauslöschliche Erinnerung in jemandes Kopf festsetzt. Auch das ist eine vertraute Erfahrung in unserem modernen Leben, denn alle unsere Erinnerungen werden in technologischen Medien für uns aufbewahrt statt in unserem Gedächtnis. Die ungeheure Menge dieses Materials verursacht uns Unbehagen.

Unsere Zeit wird von allen erdenklichen Lichtern aus der Vergangenheit beleuchtet, die bis in die abgelegensten Winkel reichen. Sie ist wie ein Raum, der vollständig in »Slow Glass« festgehalten ist. Es gibt keine Schatten, alles ist schonungslos hell.

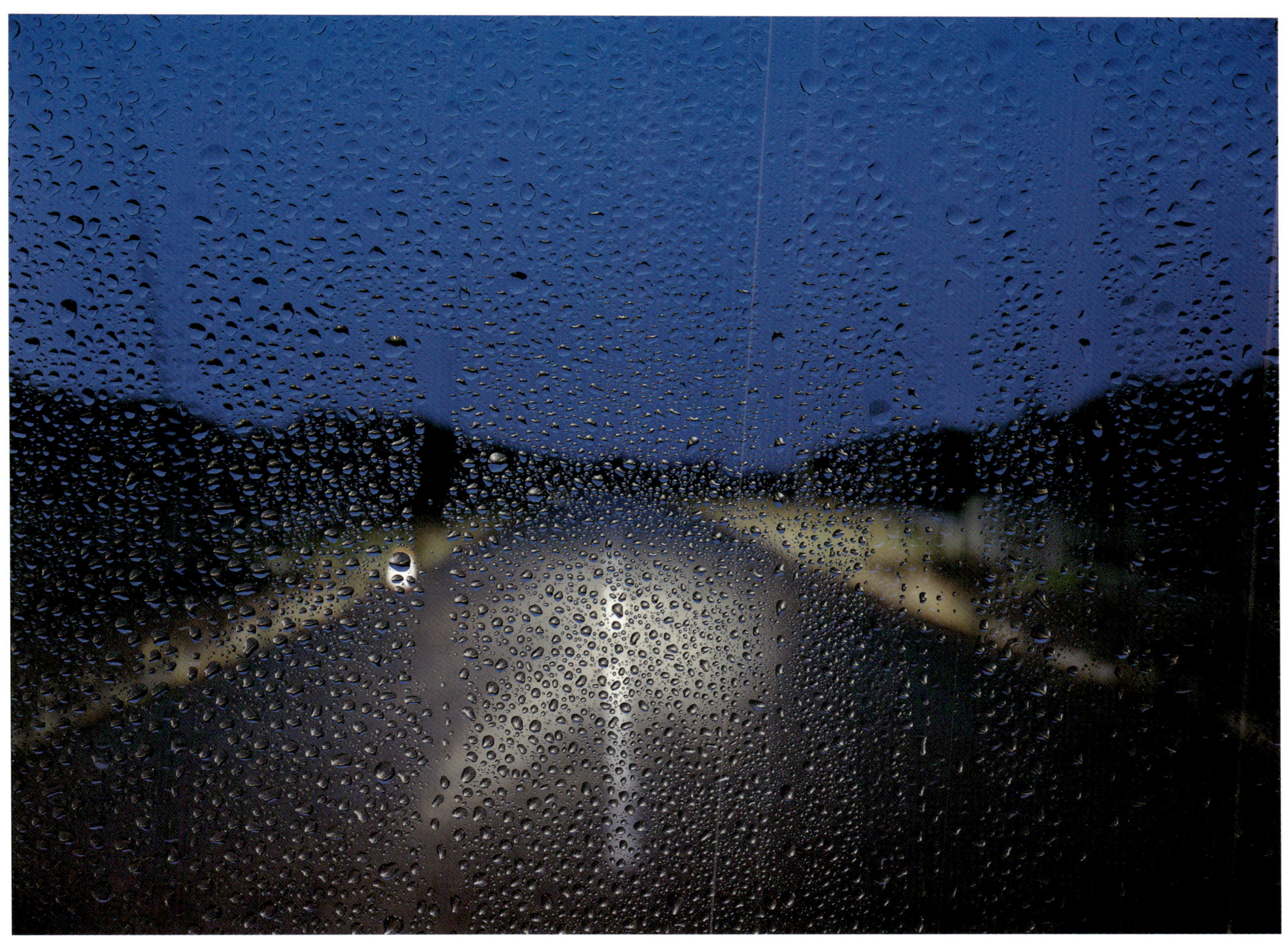

081

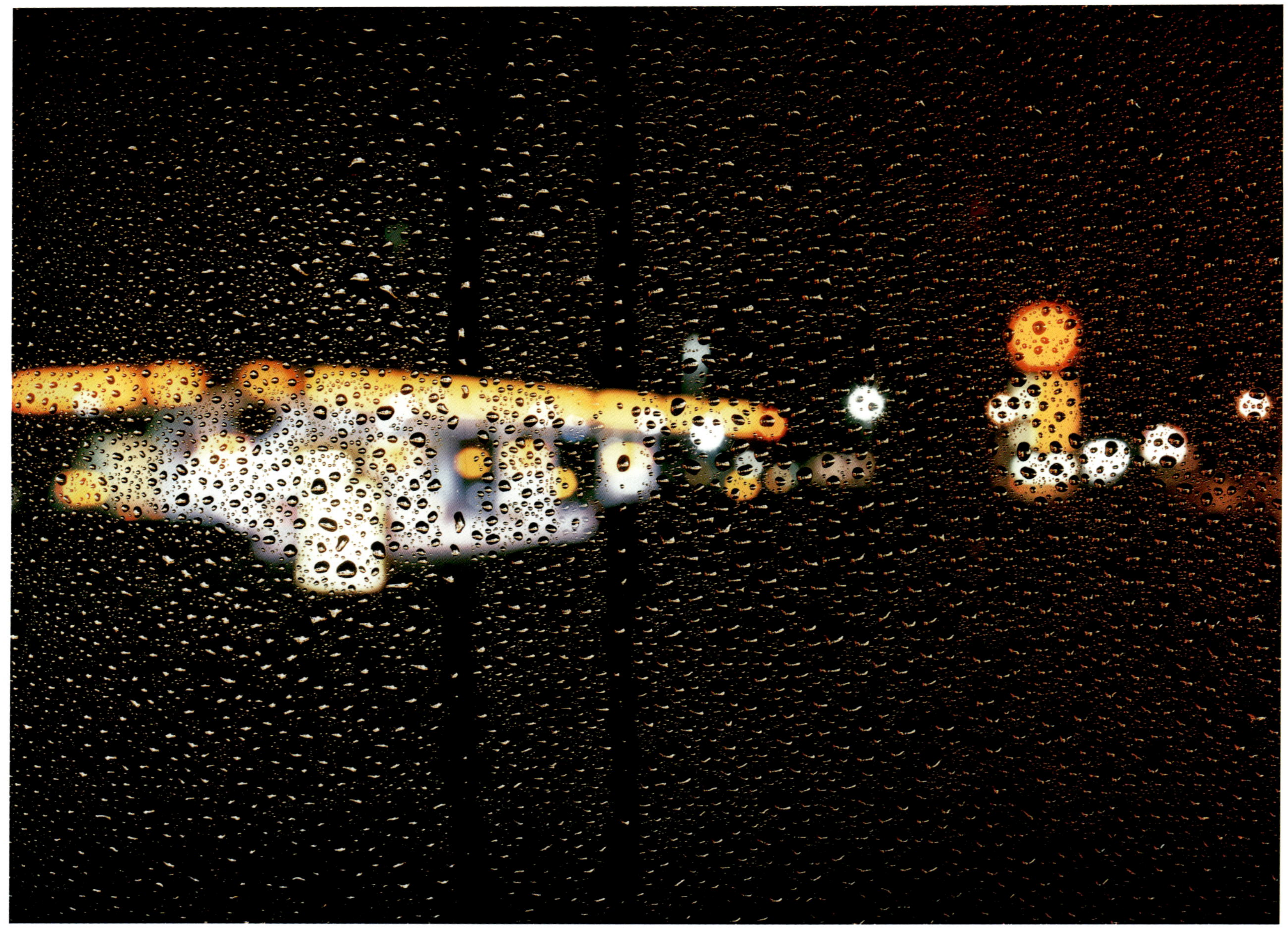

057

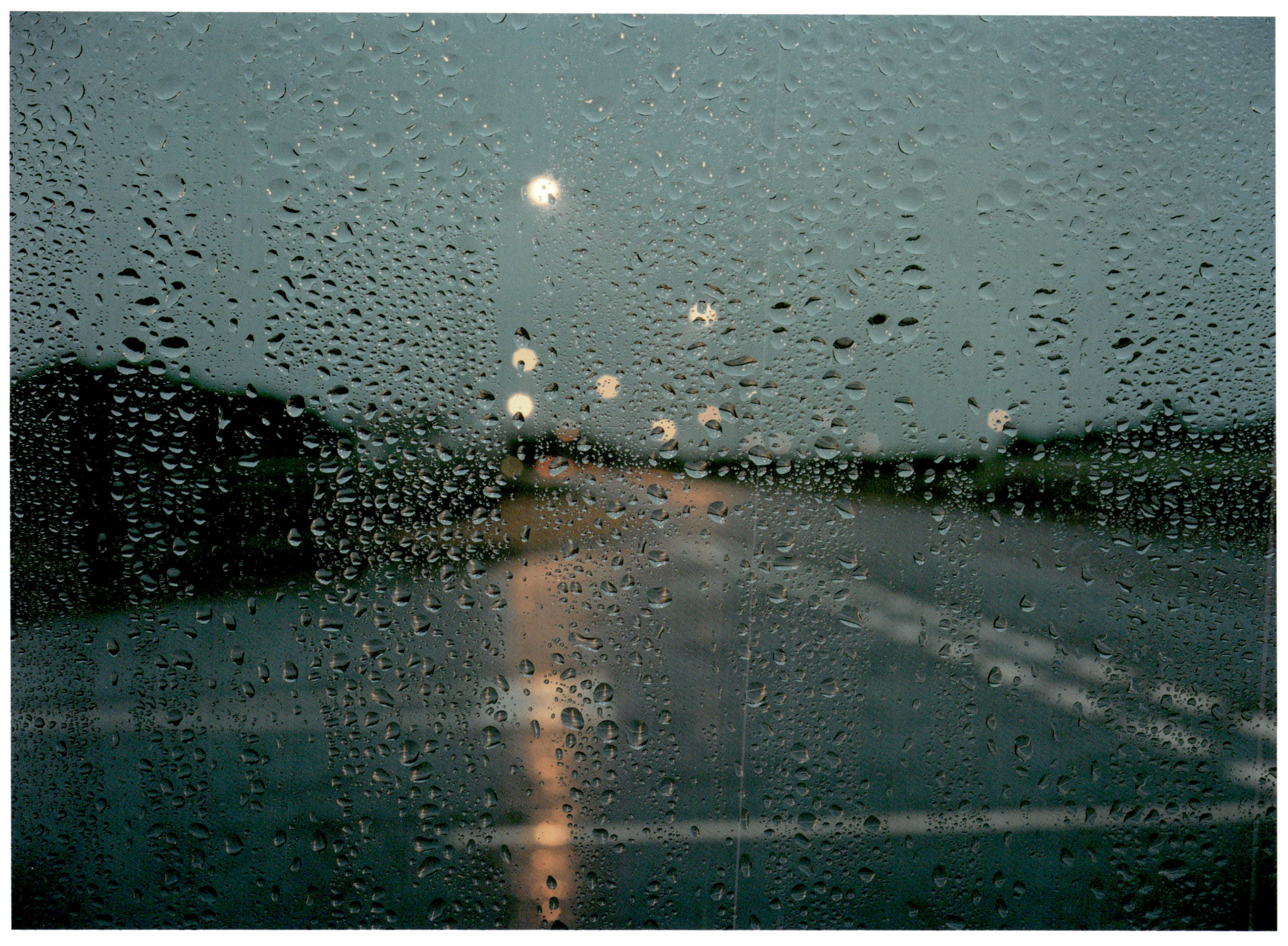

095

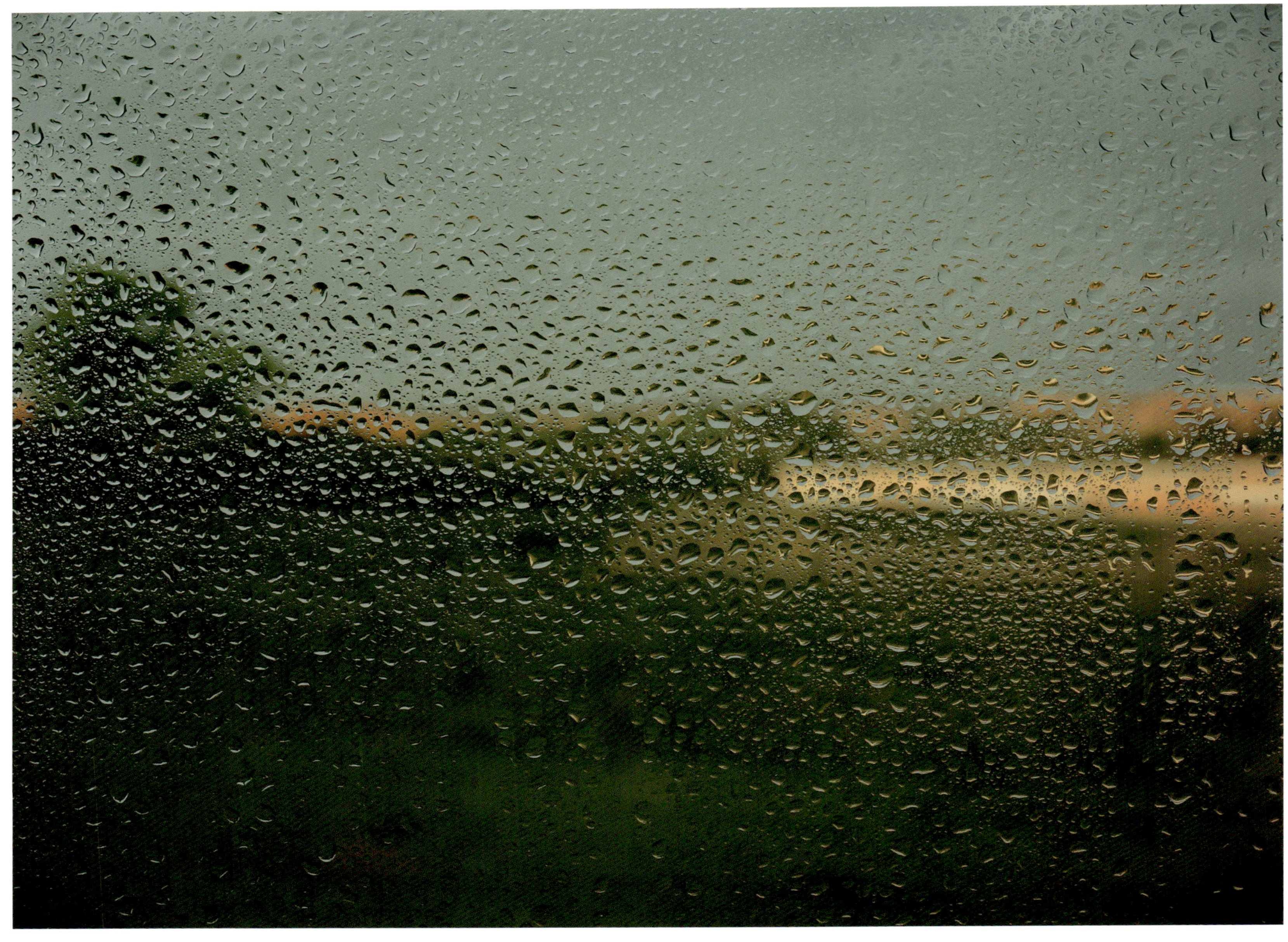

036

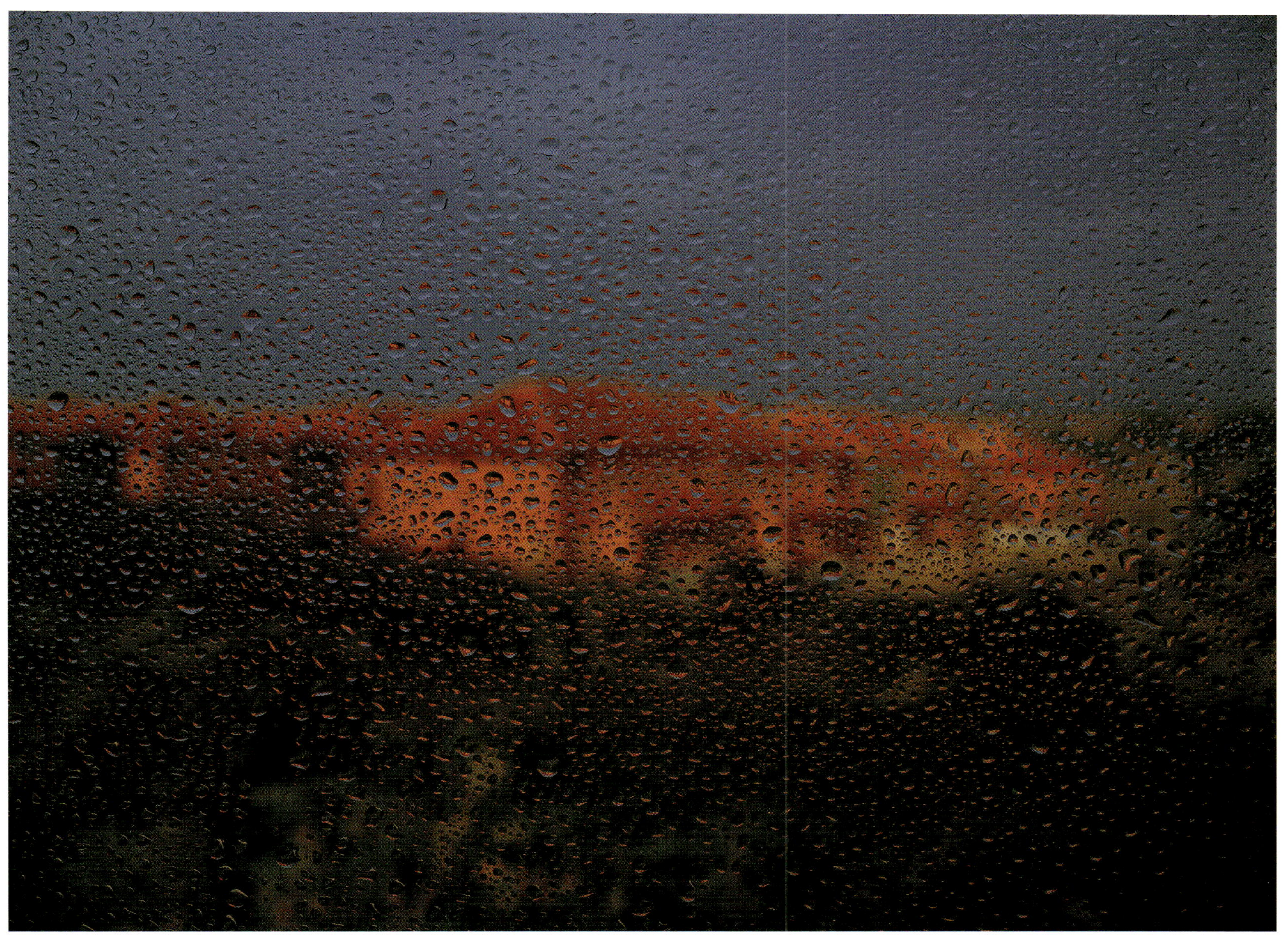

035

Away from Home

Charlotte Cotton

As part of the UK-wide *Japan 2001* festival, Naoya Hatakeyama took up a four-month artist's residency in Milton Keynes. He created two visually contrasting series of photographs during this time titled *Slow Glass* and *Still Life*, which offer a sense of his experience of the UK's most well-known new town. Naoya Hatakeyama's residency in Milton Keynes was a significant shift in the climate that he usually works. Most obviously, Hatakeyama has photographed predominantly in Japanese locations, contemplating both urban sprawl as well as dramatic sites of industrial activity and usually unseen architectural infrastructures. Naoya Hatakeyama's observations are those of a photographer who is very familiar with his surroundings and able to move beyond an initial photographic engagement into a much more abstract and detailed exploration of a place and his relationship to it. The other shift that working in Milton Keynes created was in its short timescale of four months. Hatakeyama's final resolution of a body of work is often consciously slow, completed over a number of years, and with his *Untitled* grid of panoramic views of Tokyo that he began in 1989, still ongoing. Producing work in a foreign city over a relatively short period of time was, to some degree, a liberation from his usual practice as well as a challenge to him. In an important way this residency was a sensitive and astute proposal for Hatakeyama. He has consistently worked in environments that have been or are being radically changed by architectural and industrial endeavors and his long-standing collaboration with the architect Toyo Ito bears witness to Hatakeyama's fascination for architecture.

With the architecture of domestic housing in Milton Keynes, Hatakeyama created the *Still Life* photographs. There is a wit and gentleness in Hatakeyama's approach, and both his pleasure in and ambivalence towards these sites are evident. Hatakeyama's detachment from his subject is shown by his elevated vantage point onto the clusters of red brick houses, created by placing his camera three meters from the ground. This perspective heightens the sense of the city planning of this new town, of ways of life via the architect's model or blueprint. Hatakeyama also introduces lyrical elements into *Still Life* that counteract the potentially ironic stance of these photographs. Many of the photographs are taken as the day reaches sunset, sometimes at twilight. These are times of day tinged with a Romanticism and an alchemy that are present in other aspects of these images. Hatakeyama turns flooded car parks into the village ponds of rural idylls, reflecting the façades of the modest, nearby houses. The driveways of the cul-de-sacs become the curving paths or country lanes drawn from the same photographic vocabulary of mid-19th-century photography, which Hatakeyama knows well. This Romantic sensibility is confirmed in the "still life" of building debris—the cables, cement mixers, and road cones—that are repeated through this series suggesting not only a building project as yet unfinished but the closing of an honest day's work.

The *Slow Glass* series shows Hatakeyama finding another compelling photographic strategy for his experience of Milton Keynes. These photographs are taken at night as a soft, English rain falls. They are images of a city that cannot be negotiated by foot, and Hatakeyama's response was to reflect how his car-dependent state engendered a cocooned, solitary experience of the unfamiliar city. Milton Keynes is visible in the unfocused, time-lapsed tracings of the lights of the city's buildings and traffic. It is only in the raindrops that the views are focused. Like the horizon line of his *River Series* (1993–94), there is a shifting between depth and flatness and, similarly, a liberation from photographic perspective and a loosing of oneself in the shallow planes of the images. In *River Series*, he visually "cuts" the image with a central horizon, made by aligning the banks and surface of the canal, creating a strong disturbance in the images. This rupture describes his observation of the dual momentum of the city, both upward and underground. The emphatic horizon also creates a play between the two- and three-dimensional possibilities of his photographic space and offers a way into the photograph through a single visual element that plays against a registering of the entire frame. The experience of oscillation between distance and closeness, part and whole is the dramatizing of looking that characterizes Hatakeyama's photographs and what *Slow Glass* shares with his previous series.

In *Slow Glass*, the glass surface of the camera, mimicking the glass of the car windscreen, holds the water droplets that each contain the view beyond it. A further, much more dramatic spatial play is drawn up between the glass and drops of water and the landscape in the distance. The scenes that fill the frame of these photographs are visible only from a distance and lost when contemplating the detail of the lens-covered screen. The title, *Slow Glass*, is taken from a fictional story about the invention of a magical new glass. This glass has the capacity to slow down the speed of light and keep a visual trace of the scene that passes through it. The delaying of light and holding of the image in the glass allows the view to be transported to other places and used in preference to the actual view at the new location. Hatakeyama felt an affinity between the story and the process of making the photographs in Milton Keynes as he attempted to hold in the glass his response to the city. This is the way he saw Milton Keynes behind the windscreen of his car as the rain fell and the lights from buildings and passing traffic were recorded on the slow glass of his camera.

Fern von Zuhause

Charlotte Cotton

Im Rahmen des in ganz England stattfindenden Festivals »Japan 2001« trat Naoya Hatakeyama einen viermonatigen Aufenthalt als »Artist in Residence« in Milton Keynes an. Während dieser Zeit schuf er zwei auf den ersten Blick gegensätzlich wirkende Fotoserien mit den Titeln *Slow Glass* und *Still Life*, die Eindrücke seiner Erfahrungen mit Englands bekanntester »new town« vermitteln. Naoya Hatakeyamas Aufenthalt in Milton Keynes brachte eine wesentliche Veränderung seiner sonst üblichen Arbeitsatmosphäre mit sich. Für gewöhnlich fotografiert Hatakeyama an japanischen Orten und widmet sich dabei sowohl urbanem Wildwuchs als auch spektakulären Stätten industrieller Aktivität sowie gemeinhin übersehener architektonischer Infrastruktur. Hatakeyamas Beobachtungen sind die eines mit seiner Umgebung höchst vertrauten Fotografen, der in der Lage ist, sich über anfängliches Fotografieren hinaus auf eine weit abstraktere und detailliertere Beschäftigung mit einem Ort und seiner eigenen Beziehung zu ihm einzulassen. Die zweite Veränderung, die die Arbeit in Milton Keynes mit sich brachte, betrifft die kurze Zeitspanne von vier Monaten. Hatakeyama lässt sich bei der endgültigen Fassung einer Arbeit oft bewusst Zeit, sodass die Fertigstellung eine Reihe von Jahren in Anspruch nehmen kann; an seiner *Untitled* benannten Serie mit Panoramaansichten Tokios, mit der er 1989 begann, arbeitet er noch immer. In einer fremden Stadt in relativ kurzer Zeit eine Werkreihe zu schaffen bedeutete in gewissem Sinn eine Befreiung von seiner üblichen Vorgehensweise und zugleich eine Herausforderung. Hatakeyama befasste sich auch in früheren Serien beständig mit Terrains, in denen architektonische oder industrielle Maßnahmen zu radikalen Änderungen geführt haben oder gerade führen. Auch die langjährige Zusammenarbeit mit dem Architekten Toyo Ito zeugt von Hatakeyamas ausgeprägtem Interesse an Architektur.

Für die Fotografien von *Still Life* beschäftigte sich Hatakeyama mit der Architektur einer Wohnsiedlung in Milton Keynes. Sein Vorgehen zeichnet sich durch Witz und Liebenswürdigkeit aus, und sowohl sein Vergnügen an diesen Orten als auch seine zwiespältige Haltung ihnen gegenüber werden anschaulich. Hatakeyamas Distanz zum Gegenstand wird verdeutlicht durch seine erhöhte Sicht auf die Gruppen roter Backsteinhäuser, für die er seine Kamera drei Meter über dem Boden platzierte. Diese Perspektive steigert das Empfinden für die Stadtplanung dieser »new town«, für Lebensweisen, die von Modellen und Blaupausen des Architekten verfügt werden. Außerdem ergänzt Hatakeyama *Still Life* durch lyrische Elemente, mit denen er der potenziell ironischen Aussage dieser Fotografien entgegenwirkt. Viele dieser Arbeiten entstanden während des Sonnenuntergangs, manche in der Dämmerung. Dabei handelt es sich um Tageszeiten – gefärbt von einer gewissen Romantik und Alchimie –, die auch in einem anderen Kontext dieser Bilder präsent sind. Hatakeyama verwandelt überflutete Parkplätze in Dorfteiche ländlicher Idyllen, in denen sich die Fassaden der umstehenden, einfachen Häuser spiegeln. Die Einfahrten der Sackgassen werden zu gewundenen Pfaden oder Landstraßen, die Hatakeyama aus dem gleichen, ihm gut bekannten fotografischen Vokabular um die Mitte des 19. Jahrhunderts bezieht. Diese romantische Empfindsamkeit findet Bestätigung im Stillleben aus Bauzubehör – den Kabeln, Zementmischern und Markierungshütchen –, das in der gesamten Serie vorkommt und nicht nur auf ein bislang unvollendetes Bauvorhaben schließen lässt, sondern auch auf den Abschluss eines ehrbaren Tagwerks.

In der Serie *Slow Glass* findet Hatakeyama eine weitere zwingende Fotostrategie für seine Erfahrung mit Milton Keynes. Diese Aufnahmen entstanden bei Nacht, als ein sanfter, englischer Regen fiel. Es sind Bilder einer Stadt, die sich nicht zu Fuß erschließen lässt, und Hatakeyama reagierte darauf, indem er wiedergibt, wie seine Abhängigkeit vom Auto ein Gefühl von Abschottung und Einsamkeit in der unbekannten Stadt erzeugt. Milton Keynes ist sichtbar in den unscharfen, mit dem Zeitraffer aufgenommenen Spuren der Lichter des Verkehrs und der Gebäude der Stadt. Einzig in den Regentropfen erscheinen die Ansichten scharf. Wie beim Horizont seiner *River Series* (1993/94) erfolgt eine Verschiebung zwischen Räumlichkeit und Zweidimensionalität und zudem eine Befreiung von der fotografischen Perspektive, die dazu führt, dass man sich in den flach erscheinenden Bildern verliert. In *River Series* »zerschneidet« Hatakeyama das Bild gewöhnlich durch einen zentralen Horizont, der durch die Ausrichtung der Uferzone und der Oberfläche des Kanals entsteht und starke Irritation hervorruft. Dieser Bruch beschreibt die Wahrnehmung der polaren, sowohl nach oben als auch unterirdisch wirkenden Stoßrichtung der Stadt. Der betonte Horizont erzeugt außerdem ein Spiel zwischen den zwei- und dreidimensionalen Möglichkeiten des fotografischen Raums und bietet einen Einstieg in die Fotografie über ein einzelnes, visuelles Element, das die Wahrnehmung des Gesamten erschwert. Die Erfahrung des Schwankens zwischen Distanz und Nähe, Teil und Ganzem geht einher mit der Dramatisierung des Hinschauens, die Hatakeyamas Fotografien kennzeichnet und die *Slow Glass* mit seinen früheren Serien gemein hat.

In *Slow Glass* ahmt die gläserne Oberfläche der Kamera das Glas der Windschutzscheibe nach und fängt die Wassertropfen auf, von denen jeder die dahinter liegende Aussicht enthält. Ein weiteres, noch viel dramatischeres räumliches Geschehen lässt sich zwischen dem Glas mit den Wassertropfen und der fernen Landschaft beobachten. Die Szenen auf diesen Fotografien sind nur aus einer gewissen Entfernung sichtbar und verflüchtigen sich, sobald man Einzelheiten der mit Tropfen besetzten Scheibe erfassen möchte. Der Titel *Slow Glass* ist einer Erzählung über die Erfindung eines magischen Glases entnommen. Dieses Glas hat die Eigenschaft, die Lichtgeschwindigkeit herabzusetzen und eine visuelle Spur der Szene zu bewahren, die das Glas durchdringt. Die Verzögerung des Lichts und die Konservierung des Bildes im Glas gestatten es, das Bild an andere Orte zu transportieren und es der dort tatsächlich vorhandenen Ansicht vorzuziehen. Hatakeyama verspürte in Milton Keynes eine Art Wesensverwandtschaft zwischen der Geschichte und dem Prozess des Fotografierens, und er versuchte, seine Reaktionen auf die Stadt im Glas festzuhalten. Hatakeyama nahm Milton Keynes hinter der Frontscheibe seines Autos wahr, während der Regen fiel und die Lichter von Gebäuden und vorbeifahrenden Autos auf dem »langsamen Glas« seiner Kamera festgehalten wurden.

Appendix

Biography

1958
Born in Iwate/Japan

1981
Graduated from the University of Tsukuba, School of Art & Design, Ibaraki/Japan

1984
Completed postgraduate studies at the University of Tsukuba, Ibaraki/Japan

1996
Resident artist in Djerassi Resident Artists Program, California

1997
22nd Kimura Ihei Memorial Award of Photography

2000
16th Higasikawa Domestic Photographer Prize

2001
42nd Mainichi Award of Art
Resident artist in Light Xchange, Milton Keynes/UK

Lives and works in Tokyo

Solo Exhibitions

1983
Zeit-Foto Salon, Tokyo

1986
Tokyo University of Art & Design

1987
Photo Interform, Osaka/Japan

1988
Zeit-Foto Salon, Tokyo

1989
Théâtre d'Hérouville, Caen/France

1990
Artothèque de Nantes/France
Bibliothèque de Falaise/France
Institute du Monde Arabe, Paris

1991
Photo Interform, Osaka/Japan

1994
Gallery NW House, Tokyo
Fox Talbot Museum, Lacock/UK

1996
Gallery NW House, Tokyo
Istituto Giapponese di Cultura di Roma, Rome
Centro Iniziative Multimediali Diagonale, Rome

1997
Minolta Photo Space, Tokyo, etc.

1998
Yuki Civic Center, Ibaraki/Japan
Gallery NW House, Tokyo
L.A. Galerie, Frankfurt on Main/Germany

1999
Chukyo University C-Square, Nagoya/Japan
Masataka Hayakawa Gallery, Tokyo

2000
L.A. Galerie, Frankfurt on Main/Germany
Architecture Gallery, Columbia University, New York

2001
Under Construction: Toyo Ito's Sendai Mediatheque. Photography by Naoya Hatakeyama, The AA School, London; Columbia University, New York (with Toyo Ito)

2002
Northern Gallery for Contemporary Art, Sunderland/UK
Kunstverein Hannover/Germany
Kunsthalle Nürnberg/Germany
Huis Marseille, Amsterdam
L.A. Galerie, Frankfurt on Main/Germany
Winchester Gallery/UK
Impressions Gallery, York/UK
Iwate Prefectural Museum of Art/Japan
National Museum of Art, Osaka/Japan

Group Exhibitions

1981
Camera Works, University of Tsukuba, Ibaraki/Japan

1985
Paris, New York, Tokyo, Tsukuba Museum of Photography 85, Ibaraki/Japan

1986
Fotografía japonesa contemporánea (Touring exhibition), La Casa Elizalde, Barcelona/Spain, etc.

1988
Contemporary Photographs from Japan, Columbia College, Chicago
Tama Vivant 88, Seed Hall, Tokyo

1989
The 9th Hara Annual, Hara Museum of Contemporary Art, Tokyo
Orientalism, International Design Exposition, White Museum, Nagoya/Japan

1990
A Selection of Photographs on the Sea, Shimonoseki City Art Museum, Yamaguchi/Japan
Japanese Contemporary Photography: Twelve Viewpoints, Tokyo Metropolitan Museum of Photography, Pavillon des Arts, Paris

1991
Vach'image, Maison des Jeunes et de la Culture (MJC), Saint-Gervais, Genève/Switzerland
Miyako Ishuichi, Michiko Kon, Tokihiro Sato and Nayoa Hatakeyama: Make-Believe (Touring exhibition), The Photographers' Gallery, London, etc.

1992
Matrix of Photography 3, Kawasaki City Museum, Kanagawa/Japan

1993
In die Felsen bohren sich Zikadenstimmen: Zeitgenössische japanische Photographie, Kunsthaus Zürich/Switzerland

1994
Liquid Crystal Futures (Touring in Europe and Tokyo), The Fruitmarket Gallery, Edinburgh/Scotland, etc.
Desert of Desires, Spiral Garden, Tokyo
Kawasaki Monuments, Kawasaki City Museum, Kanagawa/Japan

1995
Another Reality: Aspects of Contemporary Photography, Kawasaki City Museum, Kanagawa/Japan

1996
Land of Paradox (Touring in USA and Japan, 1996–1998), Photographic Resource Center, Boston/Massachusetts, etc.
Ideal Standard Life, Spiral Garden, Tokyo
New Japanese Photography in the 1990's: The Resonance of Unconsciousness, Yokohama Civic Art Gallery, Kanagawa/Japan

1997
Lazur (with Otani Yoshihisa), Delta Mirage, Tokyo
Lust und Leere: Japanische Photographie der Gegenwart (Touring in Europe, 1997–98), Kunsthalle Wien, Vienna, etc.
Surface Exposed: Photography in the Art of the 90s, Museum of Contemporary Art, Tokyo
Art is Fun: Ways of (Re)production, Hara Museum ARC, Shibukawa, Gunma/Japan

1998
Photography Today: The Absence of Distance, The National Museum of Modern Art, Tokyo
À prova de água, Centro Cultural de Belém, Lisbon
Asia City, The Photographers' Gallery, London
Speed, The Photographers' Gallery, London
Et Maintenant? Donai Yanen!, École Nationale Supérieure des Beaux Arts, Paris

1999
Wohin kein Auge reicht, Triennale der Photographie, Deichtorhallen, Hamburg/Germany
The Locus of Kimura Ihei Memorial Award of Photography 1975–1999, Kawasaki City Museum/Japan
Modena per la fotografia 1999, Galleria Civica di Modena/Italy
Toyo Ito: Blurring Architecture, Suermondt-Ludwig-Museum, Aachen/Germany

2000
-scape, Masataka Hayakawa Gallery, Tokyo
Serendipity: Photography, Video, Experimental Film and Multimedia Installation from Asia, The Japan Foundation Forum, Tokyo
Yume No Ato: Was vom Traum blieb – Zeitgenössische Kunst aus Japan, Haus am Waldsee, Berlin; Staatliche Kunsthalle Baden-Baden/Germany
The 16th Higasikawa Awards Exhibition, Higasikawa Cultural Gallery, Hokkaido/Japan
Landschaft in der zeitgenössischen Fotografie, Landesmuseum Oldenburg/Germany

2001
Fast and Slow, the 49th Venice Biennale, Japanese Pavilion, Venice/Italy
Out of Japan, Canon Photography Gallery, Victoria and Albert Museum, London
La espiritualidad del vacio, Fundación Bancaja, Valencia/Spain
Monet's Vermächtnis: Serie – Ordnung und Obsession, Hamburger Kunsthalle/Germany
Urban Pornography, The Artist Space, New York
New Heimat, Frankfurter Kunstverein, Frankfurt on Main/Germany
Bauart: Die Kunstsammlung der Heidelberger Zement AG, Kurpfälzisches Museum der Stadt Heidelberg/Germany

Public Collections

Huis Marseille, Foundation for Photography, Amsterdam
Refco Group Ltd., Chicago
AXA Art Versicherung AG, Cologne/Germany
DZ Bank AG, Frankfurt on Main/Germany
Barbier-Mueller, Genève/Switzerland
Heidelberger Zement AG/Germany
The Museum of Fine Arts, Houston/Texas
Obayashigumi, Japan
Kawasaki City Museum/Japan
Victoria and Albert Museum, London
Galleria Civica Modena/Italy
Artothèque de Nantes/France
The National Museum of Art, Osaka/Japan
Maison Européenne de la Photographie, Paris
De Pont Foundation for Contemporary Art, Tilburg/The Netherlands
Deutsche Bank, Tokyo
The Japan Foundation, Tokyo
Tokyo Metropolitan Museum of Photography
The National Museum of Modern Art, Tokyo
Channel 4 Television, UK
Conoco plc, UK
The Yamaguchi Prefectural Museum of Art, Yamaguchi/Japan
The Swiss Foundation for Photography, Kunsthaus Zürich/Switzerland

Selected Bibliography

1982
"Naoya Hatakeyama: Contour Line," in: *Camera Works*, 9, Tokyo

1988
Kazuko Sehji, *Tama Vivant 88*, exh. cat., Tokyo: Seed Hall
"New Wave," in: *Complete Collection of Japanese Photography*, 12, Tokyo: Shogakukan

1989
Jacques Py, *Contour Line*, exh. cat., Caen: Ardi

1990
Fuminori Yokoe, "Naoya Hatakeyama," in: *Japanese Contemporary Photography: Twelve Viewpoints*, exh. cat., Tokyo: Tokyo Metropolitan Museum of Photography

1991
David Chandler and Ruth Charity, *Miyako Ishuichi, Michiko Kon, Tokihiro Sato and Naoya Hatakeyama: Make-Believe*, exh. cat., London: The Photographer's Gallery

1993
Masafumi Fukagawa and David Streiff, *Contemporary Japanese Photography*, exh. cat., Tokyo: Tokyo Metropolitan Culture Foundation

1994

Osamu Hiraki, *Kawasaki Monuments*, exh. cat., Kawasaki: Kawasaki City Museum

Yuko Hasegawa, *Liquid Crystal Futures*, exh. cat., Edinburgh: Fruitmarket Gallery Publications

1995

Masafumi Fukagawa, *Another Reality: Aspects of Contemporary Photography 1995*, exh. cat., Kawasaki: Kawasaki City Museum

1997

Noriko Fuku, *Land of Paradox*, exh. cat., Tankosha Publishing Co., Ltd.

Naoya Hatakeyama, "Lime Works: Blasting," in: *New Japanese Photography in the 1990's: The Resonance of Unconsciousness*, exh. cat., Kanagawa: Yokohama Civic Art Gallery

Lime Works: Naoya Hatakeyama, Tokyo: Synergy Inc.

Peter Weiermair and Gerald Matt (ed.), *Lust und Leere: Japanische Photographie*, exh. cat., Zürich: Edition Stemmle

Watanabe Yohko and Hayashi Yoko, *Surface Exposed: Photography in the Art of the 90s*, Tokyo: Museum of Contemporary Art

1998

Photography Today: The Absence of Distance, exh. cat., Tokyo: The National Museum of Modern Art

1999

Peter Weiermair, "Naoya Hatakeyama. La singolarita di Hatakeyama," in: *Modena per la Fotografia 1999. Uno sguardo sul giappone*, exh. cat., Modena: Galleria Civica Modena

2000

Underground: Naoya Hatakeyama, Tokyo: Media Factory Inc.

2001

K. Berkemann, B. Dümpelmann and B. A. Matukiewicz, "Naoya Hatakeyama," in: *BauArt: Die Kunstsammlung der Heidelberger Zement AG*, exh. cat., Heidelberg: Kurpfälzisches Museum der Stadt Heidelberg

Matthias Bärmann, "Naoya Hatakeyama," in: *La espiritualidad del vacio*, exh. cat., Valencia: Fundación Bancaja

Naoya Hatakeyama & Toyo Ito: Under Construction, Tokyo: Kenchiku Shiryo Kenkyusha

Christoph Heinrich, "Naoya Hatakeyama. *Untitled*, 1989–1997," in: *Monets Vermächtnis: Serie – Ordnung und Obsession*, exh. cat., Ostfildern-Ruit: Hatje Cantz Publishers

Visionaire 36 Power, New York: Visionaire Publishing

La Biennale di Venezia. 49. exposizione internazionale d'arte, Milano: Electa

2002

Marc Haworth-Booth, "Slow Glass and Still Life," in: *Slow Glass: Naoya Hatakeyama*, Southampton: Light Xchange and the Winchester Gallery

Philippe Forest, "Tokyo Mythologies: Araki et Hatakeyama," in: *Artpress*, 275, Paris

Catalogue

Catalogue to accompany the exhibition
"Naoya Hatakeyama"
Kunstverein Hannover, 13. 4. 2002 – 19. 5. 2002
Kunsthalle Nürnberg, 25. 7. 2002 – 15. 9. 2002
Huis Marseille, Amsterdam,
30. 11. 2002 – 23. 2. 2003

The artist would like to thank
Lothar Albrecht, L.A. Galerie, Frankfurt on Main
Susie Medley, Light Xchange
Corinne Quentin
Akiko Tobu

Editor: Stephan Berg

Editing: Ute Barba, Silke Boerma, Tas Skorupa
Assistance: Angela Lautenbach

Translation into English:
John S. Southard (Stephan Berg)

Translation into German: Christiane Court
(Charlotte Cotton), Christoph Hollender
(Statements Naoya Hatakeyama)

Graphic design and typesetting:
Gabriele Sabolewski

Reproduction: Repromayer, Reutlingen

Printed by: Dr. Cantz'sche Druckerei,
Ostfildern-Ruit/Germany

Cover illustration: *Untitled/Osaka*, 1998–99,
2 C-Prints, mounted on aluminum,
89 x 180 cm (each), Courtesy L.A. Galerie,
Frankfurt on Main; the artist

Published by
Hatje Cantz Verlag
Senefelderstraße 12
73760 Ostfildern-Ruit / Germany
Tel. 0049/711/44050
Fax 0049/711/4405220
www.hatjecantz.de

Distribution in the US
D.A.P., Distributed Art Publishers, Inc.
155 Avenue of the Americas, Second Floor
New York, N.Y. 10013-1507
USA
Tel. 001/212/6271999
Fax 001/212/6279484

ISBN 3-7757-1159-7
Printed in Germany

Die Deutsche Bibliothek – CIP-Einheitsaufnahme

Naoya Hatakeyama ; Kunstverein Hannover
vom 13. April bis 19. Mai 2002 ; Kunsthalle
Nürnberg vom 25. Juli bis 15. September 2002 ;
Huis Marseille, Amsterdam vom 30. November
2002 bis 23. Februar 2003 / Stephan Berg ;
Charlotte Cotton. Hrsg.: Stephan Berg. – Ost-
fildern-Ruit : Hatje Cantz, 2002
ISBN 3-7757-1159-7